INTEGRATED LIBRARY MANAGEMENT SYSTEMS:
An Indian Scenario of Modern Library Automation

INTEGRATED LIBRARY MANAGEMENT SYSTEMS:

An Indian Scenario of Modern Library Automation

By

Hilal Ahmad

joeme198@live.com

drhilal@kashmiruniversity.ac.in

Ess Ess Publications

New Delhi

INTEGRATED LIBRARY MANAGEMENT SYSTEMS:
An Indian Scenario of Modern Library Automation

ISBN: 978-81-7000-810-1

First Published 2016

Published by:
Ess Ess Publications
4831/24, Ansari Road,
Darya Ganj,
New Delhi-110 002.
INDIA
Phones: 23260807, 41563444
Fax: 41563334
E-mail: info@essessreference.com
www.essessreference.com

Cover Design by *Patch Creative Unit*

Printed and bound in India at Salasar Imaging Systems.

Dedicated
To
My Loving Mother & Father
FATIMA & GH. AHMAD

Contents

Preface

The technological applications in libraries for their effective and efficient operations to serve their users in a better way have been long sought professional literature on library automation. Initially library automation received cold response in India, however, with the falling price of hardware's, easy availability of library softwares and ever-increasing interest among the librarians, Indian academic libraries are witnessing a tremendous transition from manual system to automated system of information access. Nevertheless, the selection of appropriate software package for effectively automating library operations and services has been a challenging task for Indian librarians. Even though a number of indigenous library softwares were developed, but only few of them survived, while the rest did not last long due to their shortcomings in compatibility with the international standards.

In-spite of the fact that the initiative of UGC to provide adequate grants and development of SOUL software by INFLIBNET for automating College and University libraries paved the way for automating their operations and services, nevertheless, the technological scenario of most of the academic libraries is not encouraging. Besides this, the implementation of integrated library softwares also demand detailed training of librarians for thorough change in their work environment. Owing majorly to the shortcomings of indigenous packages, many Indian libraries switched over to foreign software packages.

In this backdrop, this book presents a detailed description of library automation from its historic to modern period both at Indian as well as at global level. The book throws thorough light on present picture of automated library system of academic and special libraries with particular mention of College and University Libraries of India. Besides discussing the different modules of softwares and the user satisfaction with the automated library system, the book also highlights the expertise of librarians in managing the automated library systems. Since an effort has been made to highlight many issues and complexities faced by the Indian librarians in automating libraries, it is therefore, expected that this book will serve as an aiding tool for university and college librarians in selecting appropriate integrated library management system for effective and efficient automation of their operations and services.

— *Hilal Ahmad*

Acknowledgements

On earth, nothing is possible without the help and will of the 'Creator' of universe, Who created man by an ordinary clot, then taught him to explore nature, by learning from cradle to grave, which he knew not, by using pen against sword. I would primarily use my pen for paying eternal gratitude to Almighty Allah, Who blessed me with the pre-requisite patience and strength to accomplish this book.

The gratitude next in line be to my Teacher Prof. Mehtab Alam Ansari, Department of Library and Information Science, Aligarh Muslim University who in-spite of his own commitments to academics and awful family tragedies, always stood by me during the course of my research study. Being an expert in library automation, he provided me the required guidance, support and encouragement at every point of time. I may also point out here that there are many to teach you academics, but few, who besides academics teach you the morality, respect, values, obligation and punctuality. My teacher has been an example in all these respects.

This book undoubtedly bears the impression of everlasting love of my family. I feel short of vocabulary to pen down the most appropriate words of my gratitude and devotion to my parents. Indebtedness is beyond words to my Father Mr. Gh, Ahmad and Mother Fatima, who have been bone marrow of my all time studies. My word of gratitude is also due to my brothers and sisters who have been pillars of my strength all the way.

At the backend, there is someone special, who has been the cause and source of my academic writing. She has been the first by whom and for whom; I undertook this effort. During the entire course of scripting, my *"Beloved"* has whole heartedly sacrificed her share of my time and has been building block of my moral back-up and keystone of my strength, patience and courage at every thick and thin.

I sincerely express my profound gratitude to Prof. A. M. Baba, University Librarian and Head, Library and Information Science, University of Kashmir for his nonstop inspiration for modelling my higher studies.

There are no curtains on the feelings and gratitude to many unmentioned persons due to shrinking of space; I offer my sincere thanks to all of them.

I hope this book makes a substantial contribution to library automation and integrated library management systems particularly in developing countries.

— *Hilal Ahmad*

Abbreviations Used

AACR	Anglo American Cataloguing Rules
AICTE	All India Council of Technical Education
ALS	Automated Library System
AMC	Annual Maintenance Contract
AMS	American Mathematical Society
AMU	Aligarh Muslim University
AOL	America On-line
ARPAnet	Advanced Research Project Agency Network
ASCII	American Standard Code of Information Interchange
ASTM	Asynchronous Transfer Mode
ATM	Automated Teller Machine
BALLOTS	Bibliographic Automation of Large Library Operations
BARC	Baba Atomic Research Center
BLBSD	British Library Bibliographic Services Division
BRS	Bibliographic Retrieval Services
CALIBNET	Calcutta Library and Information Network
CANMARC	Canadian Machine Readable Catalogue Records
CARS	Computer Aided Reference Service

CAS	Current Awareness Services
CCF	Common Communication Format
CD-ROM	Compact Disc Read Only Memory
CDS/ISIS	Computerized Documentation System/ Integrated Set for Information Systems
CLSI	Computer Library System Inc
CMC	Computer Maintenance Corporation
CRT	Cathode Ray Tube
DELMS	Defense Library Management System
DELNET	Developing Libraries Network
DESIDOC	Defense Science Information and Documentation Center
DRDO	Defense Research and Development Organization
EDI	Electronic Data Interchange
E-Journals	Electronic Journals
E-mail	Electronic Mail
ERL	Electronic Reference Library
ERNET	Educational and Research Network
ESA/IRS	European Space Agency's Information Retrieval Service
ETD	Electronic Theses and Dissertations
FRBR	Functional Requirement for Bibliographic Records.
FTP	File Transfer Protocol
GAT	General Aptitude Test
GUI	Graphical User Interface
IBERMARC	Spanish version of MARC
IBM	International Business Machine
IAS	Indian Administrative Service
ICT	Information Communication Technology

IGNOU	Indira Gandhi National Open University
IIM	Indian Institute of Management
IIPM	Indian Institute of Petroleum Management
IIT	Indian Institute of Technology
IISc	Indian Institute of Science
IOC	Indian Oil Corporation
ILL	Inter Library Loan
ILS	Integrated Library Systems
ILMS	Integrated Library Management Systems
INDEST	Indian National Digital Library in Engineering Sciences and Technology
INFLIBNET	Information and Library Network
INSDOC	Indian National Scientific and Documentation Center
INSPEC	International Information Services to Physics and Engineering Communities
IOS	Information Outlets
IR	Institutional Repository
ISA	Indian Science Abstract
ISBD	International Standard Bibliographic Description
ISI	Indian Statistical Institute
ISO	International Organization for Standardization
ISPs	Internet Service Providers
IT	Information Technology
IITK	Indian Institute of Technology, Kanpur
IIT-KLAS	IIT-Kanpur Library Automation Software
JANET	Joint Academic and Research Network
JCCC	J-Gate Custom Content for Consortia
J-Gate	Journal Gate

JNU	Jawaharlal Nehru University
JSTOR	Journal Storage Archive
KAS	Kashmir Administrative Service
KLIBNET	Kashmir Library Network
KWIC	Keyword-in-Context
KWAC	Keyword-Augmented-Context
KWOC	Keyword-Out-of Context
LAN	Local Area Network
LCSH	Library of Congress Subject Headings
LIBRIS	Library Information System
LISA	Library and Information Science Abstracts
LLSAPs	Local Library System Automation Projects
MAN	Metropolitan Area Network
MARC	Machine Readable Catalogue Records
Mbps	Mega Bits Per Second
MS-DOS	Micro Soft Disc Operating System
MSN	Microsoft Network
MY SQL	My Structured Query Language
NBHM	National Board of Higher Mathematics
NET	National Eligibility Test
NICEE	National Information Centre of Earthquake Engineering
NICNET	National Information Center Network
NISO	National Information Standards Organization
NISSAT	National Information System for Science and Technology
NLM	National Library of Medicine
NOTIS	Northwestern On-line Total Integrated System
NUCSSI	National Union Catalogue of Scientific Serials in India

OAR	Open Access Resources
OCLC	Online Computer Library Center
OPAC	On-line Public Access Catalogue
PCs	Personal Computers
PDF	Portable Document Format
PhD	Doctor of Philosophy
PG	Post Graduate
PGDLAN	Post Graduate Diploma in Library Automation and Networking
PUNNET	Pune Library Network
R&D	Research and Development
RAM	Random Access Memory
RDA	Resource Description and Access
RDBMS	Relational Database Management System
RFID	Radio Frequency Identification
RLG	Research Libraries Group
RLIN	Research Libraries Information Network
RSS	Really Simple Syndicate
SAARC	South Asian Association for Regional Cooperation
SDI	Selective Dissemination of Information
SEWMARC	Swedish Machine Readable Catalogue Records
SGML	Standard Generalized Mark Language
SIRNET	Scientific and Industrial Research Network
SMS	Short Message Service
SOUL	Software for University Libraries
TB	Tera Byte
TCP/IP	Transmission Control Protocol/ Internet Protocol
TIFR	Tata Institute of Fundamental Research

TOEFL	Test Of English and Foreign Languages
TULIPS	Tata Unisys Library Information Processing System
UGC	University Grants Commission
UGC-INFONET	UGC Information Network
UK	United Kingdom
UKMARC	United Kingdom Machine Readable Catalogue Records
UNESCO	United Nations Educational Scientific and Cultural Organization
UNIMARC	Universal Machine Readable Catalogue Records
UPSC	Union Public Service Commission
URL	Uniform Resource Locator
US	United States
USA	United States of America
USMARC	United States Machine Readable Catalogue Records
USSR	Union Soviet Socialist Russia
UTLAS	University of Toronto Library Automation Systems
VCP	Video Cassette Player
V-SAT	Very Small Aperture Terminal
VSNL	Videsh Sanchar Nigam Limited
VTLS	Virginia Technology Library Solutions
WLN	Washington Library Network
WSU	Washington State University
WWW	World Wide Web
XML	Extensible Mark Language

List of Figures

List of Tables

application introduced off line batch processing in libraries to enhance acquisition, cataloguing, circulation and serial control sections. By the mid 60s, more than 80 American academic libraries which shortly extended to 150 libraries, computerized their circulation system. Similarly, acquisition section was also computerized. During early 60s, libraries like University of California and San Diego attempted to go beyond the listing of serials by implementing procedures for check-in and claiming (Salmon, 1969). One of the most important landmarks of this decade was the evolution of Library of Congress MARC format.

The decreasing size and price of computers lead to the development of mini- computers. The emergence of mini computers ushered libraries in the era of online automation as discussed earlier. Between late 60s and 80s, three trends like in-house projects, bibliographic utilities and pre packaged Turnkey automated systems evolved in the development of online library system. The first of such system was Illinois State Library System. In 1967, Midwestern University in Wichita Falls Texas implemented online circulation system and in 1968, the Booth Library at Eastern Illinois University in Charleston operated its own version of online circulation system. In the same year, Washington State University (WSU) library designed acquisition system, while university of Laval in Quebec set up online serials control system. By the decade of 70s, a number of academic libraries begun to incorporate mini computers in their circulation operations. The outstanding example was that of Ohio State University that facilitated users to search the item by call numbers, title key and a combination of author title key (Reynolds, 1985).

There were other large research libraries interested in online integrated system during this period, but actual implementation could be done only after several years of proper design, careful planning and experimentation. The

1

Background and Beginning of Library Automation

The main objective of this chapter is to give an outline and efforts undertaken and the key factors that were influential in the inception of Library Management Systems at National and International level. The chapter begins with the introduction explaining the background information; concept and definitions. The chapter further details about the scenario of automation in United States, Europe and developing countries with special reference to India. It also discusses the resource sharing through automation.

INTRODUCTION

The term library is understood to have been reaped from the Latin word *'liber'* connoting book(s) placed in an organized manner for the purpose of use. The term traces its lineage back to preservation of written records to preserve human communication and is considered to have begun in the historic age. Historically, it is assumed to be a collection of graphic materials arranged for easy use, taken care of by an individual(s), familiar with that arrangement and available for use by at least some persons. However with the trends of time, libraries turned to an organized collection of general information and literature for the purpose of their utilization (Johnson, 1965). Earlier libraries were thought to be responsible for harbouring the functions of collection, organization and circulation of their meagre sources and services, but the phenomenal progress in technology and exponential growth in literature made it obligatory for librarians to adopt new techniques and technology for modern libraries in order to cope up with the varied emerging circumstances.

Like any other field, libraries were also at the threshold of Information Communication Technology (ICT). The developments of this technology made the role of otherwise unused libraries, multi focal and multipurpose. Since centuries libraries have been most vibrant agents in transforming knowledge usually organized in print form, however, the application of machines to process and transfer this knowledge in a better way represents modernization of libraries. Modernization, nonetheless, with itself brings the new challenges that creates issues and concerns and lay added stress on any questionable area of prevailing structures. Although, there is high degree of cooperation between the prevailing and current technology primarily dominated with the computers, but the later one has an advantage over the old as it is equipped with qualities that better accommodate current circumstances (Webb, 1987).

The introduction of computers in various sections of libraries such as acquisition; cataloguing; circulation and periodicals offered libraries a new look. The primary interest of automating such operations does not stand for elimination of man in favour of machines, but the choice of both in the tasks best suited to each. Computer technology offered hardware and software and conceptual foundations to build automated library system, where optimum use of man and machines is put into practice to enhance the library operations and services (Heiliger & Henderson, 1971). Thus technology, hardware and software only provide a sketch that frames automation, but does not imply elimination of manual effort in libraries for disseminating knowledge. Automating rather, is primarily aimed at effective and efficient utilization of resources in minimum duration with least cost and effort, yielding maximum output and benefits both for library and their patrons.

Since, technology has been producing wonders and will perhaps continue to renew and redefine every discipline and activity. Similarly, the unending development of computer technology brought library world to a new horizon where user friendly and economically flexible software packages are readily available; thereby, making librarians judicious to compare the strengths and shortfalls of different library management packages and choose the package for installation that is most appropriate to suit the requirement of both libraries and their end users.

ORIGIN

Library automation refers to a technical phenomenon of computerizing or automating the traditional library activities and services such as acquisition; cataloguing; circulation; serial control; information services and other related activities. Thus, the application of computers to perform various routine operations and repetitive clerical functions of libraries in an efficient and automatic manner is called as library automation.

In this direction, librarians have practiced with technological devices throughout 20th century to help libraries in improving their in-house operations and services to their patrons. Library automation has been exploited both narrowly and broadly to the devices and efforts that consolidate the foothold of technology in library operations and services. Some have paralleled it with library mechanization while others used automation in the context of close co-operation of computers and libraries. Library automation as known now, has come a long way since mechanical devices notably typewriters, telegraphs, telephones and other accessories followed by punched cards and sorters were exercised in libraries. The purpose of applying these accessories was to eliminate the burden of muscle movement in libraries, while the revolution that computers had in other fields was left to be realized in future. However, the elevation in mechanization and simultaneously the development in computer and communication technology steadily replaced the application of mechanical accessories with computers. Significantly, the growing exercise of computers in libraries restructured and remodelled their operations and services (Wedgeworth, 1993).

The origin of automation has a long history. The early Greeks, seeking freedom from the routine toil and drudgery of labor conceived of devices that might take over certain tasks. The word automation has been derived from Greek word 'automatos' meaning "self acting". It refers to an apparatus, process, or system that is capable of operating by itself in an unassisted manner (Savage, 1996). Library automation is the performance of an operation, a series of operations, or a process by self activating, self controlling, or automatic means. Automation implies the use of automatic data processing equipment such as computer or other labour saving devices (Young, 1983). While mechanization eliminated the muscle movement in libraries, automation on the other hand exploited machines in process and transmission of information. The remarkable progress in computer technology resulted in the development of more efficient hardware and software. The application of such hardware and software in libraries differentiated the concept of library automation and served as a breakthrough in processing and communicating information in a networked environment.

DEFINITIONS

Though there is globally no accepted connotation of library automation as some people call it as mechanization some computerization, while some prefer to recognize it as automation. Nevertheless due to its broad spectrum of coverage, library automation has been variously defined by number of authors, the notable among these are encapsulated hereunder:

The New Oxford American Dictionary (2001) is of the view that automation is "the use of largely automatic equipment in a system manufacturing or other production processes".

The New Encyclopaedia Britannica (1973) visualizes automation as a system in which there is significant substitution of mechanical, electrical or computerized action for human effort and intelligence and put forth an operation is commonly described as automated, if it is substantially more automatic than its predecessor.

In the opinion of (Swihart, Stanley & Hefley, 1973) library automation is the processing of certain routine clerical functions in the library with the assistance of computers or other mechanized or semi-automatic equipment.

Another scholar (Halsey, 1987) in Collier's Encyclopaedia reflects library automation to industrial movement that started in US in early 1950's and defined it as a concept of production (integration of machine tools into a fully automatic and in some cases self regulatory system) automation which he defines as means considerably more than the clever coordination of a series of machines.

In his view (Wedgeworth, 1993) envisions Library automation as a "term applied both broadly and narrowly to the tools and activities that incorporate technologies into library operations and services".

In the work of (Dutta, 1993), "Library automation" has been defined as "computerization of housekeeping activities and information retrieval function generally carried out by a library".

However (Bazirjian, 1995), visualizes library automation as the migration to second generation library system.

Library automation as per (Tyre, 1995) is a "flexible new muscle" extending its reach and making connection.

Similarly (Head & McCabe, 1996) connote library automation as the flexibility of a system that managements can choose to use them in ways that occurred with their wishes.

Zubbof, however, is of the view that library automation is a process that helps to reduce various library operations to the smallest possible components.

In their opinion (Cohn, L. Kelsey & Keith, 2002), library automation no longer reflects only to computerize operations in a discrete, physical place, but has assumed a wide frame of reference namely that of enabling the library user to reach beyond what is merely local to an information and knowledge base that is truly global and interconnected.

In the International Encyclopaedia of Information and Library Science (Feather & Sturges, 2003), library automation is taken as a blurring of the notion of the library collections as seen as located in physical place.

The design and implementation of ever more sophisticated computer systems to accomplish tasks originally done by hand in libraries is what Reltz (2004) feels about library automation.

Afterwards, the invention of mechanical means like telegraph and typewriters followed by the major breakthrough of punched cards and sorters, improved the otherwise limited functions and services of libraries. The application of these mechanical devices played a key role in attracting wide attention of users towards libraries. Henceforth, the accomplishment of manual operations and services by mechanical accessories forged the new concept that came to be known as library mechanization.

Library mechanization was endeavoured at handling complications and burdens of bulk, weight and distance at redeeming muscle and movement with machine, while automation is the name given to automatic or self controlling system of working environment (Riaz, 1992). Viewed on this background, mechanization is practicing with mechanical devices with chief intervention of mental and manual effort to accomplish repetitive clerical activities and services of libraries. However due to its shortfalls, it could not sustain for long, but paved the way for the development of an advanced concept of library computerization. The advancement in communication technology, computer hardware and software packages globalized library computerization which often in modern terminology is taken as library automation.

Library automation is an automatic or semi-automatic means of processing certain clerical functions, operations and services with the patronage and support of computers; hardwares; softwares; online products; CD-ROMs and LANs; etc. (Swihart & Hefley, 1973). Against this background, library automation differs from that of mechanization, in a way, where in place of principal intervention of manual and mechanical effort, computer systems; hardwares; softwares; communications facilities; online and networked environment etc. are practiced to execute different library operations and services.

GENESIS

Libraries have long sought technological aids to facilitate and enhance their services and to provide broader and more convenient access to traditional form of information processing. The impact of automaton on librarianship has long been an inviting subject in the professional literature. In this regard, the innovations ranging from printing press to typewriters and then to micro computers had affected wide spectrum of library operations and services which extended from the description of an item to its circulation

(Voight, 1956). Though, automation in libraries is actually said to have begun in 1930s with the use of punch cards in circulation and acquisition sections. However, the focus of this period was that information could be stored and re-used and that machines could take these punch cards and can be programmed to perform predetermined operations. The overall automation had begun with a librarian 'Herman Hollerith' of US Census bureau who invented punched cards which were first used in University of Texas for circulation control. Another development in this direction was book charging machine used by Montclair Public Library in 1942 in New Jersey.

This was followed by the development of book catalogue by Library of Congress in 1950 with the aid of punched cards, but till 1960 most of these were used in special libraries. During the decade of 60s, a small number of universities, corporate and large public libraries in US and UK put their efforts in the development of in-house library automated system. This period gained the idea of computers in libraries and led to the momentum of library automation in 60s and 70s. In the year 1961, HP Luhn experimented computers in libraries to provide Keyword-in-Context (KWIC) index for articles in Chemical Abstracts. In the same decade, libraries ushered in the era of standards for exchange of data. By the mid 60s, Library of Congress used computers for producing Machine Readable Catalogue Records (MARC) with the purpose of creating bibliographic databases of library catalogues, which led to the development and adoption of MARC practices and established shared cataloguing cooperatives (Saffady, 1989). Quickly after MARC, Library of Congress begun MARCI followed by MARC II project for venturing in shared cataloguing among a number of US libraries.

With the substantial increase in the use of micro computers, the commercial system for searching reference database such as DIALOG and bibliographic retrieval services begun. By the early 70s, some major breakthrough like Online Computer Library Centre (OCLC's) cataloguing project which went online in 1971 and similar project by University of Toronto Library Automation Systems (UTLAS) occurred in library technology. The OCLC's project was remarkable development that facilitated technical processing in library system. Few years later, Bibliographic Automation of Large Library Operations (BALLOTS) laid foundation for Research Libraries Group (RLG) which formed Research Libraries Information Network (RLIN). Similarly, another regional network Washington Library Network (WLN) got established to serve the same purpose (Riggs, 1992).

These BALLOTS were designed to integrate closely with technical processing of library and contained wide search and retrieval capability by using truncated words, keywords and Library of Congress Subject Headings (LCSH). The decade of 70s, brought another trend in library automation which consisted growth of storage capability; expansion of telecommunication capability and development of computer industry. This decade also witnessed the emergence of other online networks like RLIN, WLN and development of In-house circulation and existence of 'Turnkey' systems that allowed libraries to obtain hardware and software from vendors for automating their library systems (Reynolds, 1985).

After ushering in an online era, a range of online services became available offering access from a computer terminal in library to bibliographic databases on remote computers. In 1974, another significant development took place when MARCII became basis of a standard, incorporated by National Information Standards Organization (NISO) USA. During the same period, US Department of Defence and Advanced Research Agency developed ARPAnet to link centres working on military research. By the end of year, computers at the University of California and University of Utah were connected to

ARPAnet. In the following year, the University College of London and Norwegian Royal Radar Establishment became first international sites to connect ARPAnet. The original applications of ARPAnet were Telnet, FTP and email for exchanging messages. The recognition of usefulness of sending messages by people among themselves metamorphosed email into "Internet". Though it may not have been ARPAnet's main priority, but it ensured that internet became entrenched in the daily lives of millions of persons (Keefer & Tomas, 2001). It has been in 80s that automation has become feasibility, rather than a goal for future for large number of libraries.

With the rapid development of low cost micro computers, library automation during 80s became possible for all sizes of libraries. At the same time, technology provided faster chips, additional Random Access Memory (RAM) and storage capacity leading to decrease in the size of computers which expanded the use of micro computers tremendously into home, schools, libraries and offices. A significant invention has been online public access catalogue which replaced card catalogue in the early 80s (Riggs, 1992). By the same decade, a number of automation packages became commercially available for standard functioning of acquisition, cataloguing, circulation and serials control, all in one software package which helped to spread library automation in countries other than US and UK. The micro computers of 80s became useful tool for libraries, which put them to use from word processing to reference, circulation and serials.

With the rise of computer networking by late 80s and early 90s, libraries begun to set up and purchase their own computers as well as to connect with other established networks. Many of these networks were not developed by librarians, but by vendors, who supplied libraries with systems from cataloguing to circulation. Moreover, various application softwares like spreadsheets; word processing; data managers; dBase; Lotus 1-2-3; desktop publishing and searching for information through CD-ROMs became common during this period (Wallace & Joan, 1989). By the introduction of CD-ROMs containing softwares and databases, libraries in late 80s gained information in variety of options and remain connected to outside databases such as OCLC, DIALOG and RLIN. In this decade, information through CD-ROMs became more accessible than previously possible through print. Now, widely utilized by libraries of all types and sizes, online search services are divided into multidisciplinary services that include DIALOG; BRS; ORBIT; WILSONLINE; DATASTAR and ESAIRS. These provide data range of varied range of subjects for broad clientele and specialized services like National Library of Medicine (NLM) search service, STN International; LEXIS and WESTLAW that provide online access to one or more databases relevant to a single subject discipline, profession or activity (Saffady, 1989).

The surfacing of internet revolutionized communications in academic and research communities in the developed world by about 1990. But, its main breakthrough into the wider world appeared in mid 1990s with the development of World Wide Web. The emergence of private sector Internet Service Providers (ISPs) was another aspect of cyber revolution of late 1990s. From 1995 onwards, the Microsoft Network (MSN) was integral part of Windows operating system which dominated the personal computer market around the world. The companies such as Freeserve in UK and America Online (AOL) in USA were competitors in this direction (Feather, 2004).

The decade of 90s saw significant development in library automation systems. It is by this decade that widespread use of computers and internet was witnessed in libraries. Wider choice integrated library systems consisting acquisition; cataloguing; circulation; serials control and OPAC modules were offered by vendors. The training and maintenance services provided by these vendors further eased automating library procedure. By this decade, the use of networks for e-mail; ftp; telnet; internet and connections to online commercial systems saw remarkable growth. The World Wide Web (WWW) begun to use at large scale and libraries became able to connect to inter library loan systems with ever improving telecommunications. With speedy growth, expert systems and knowledge systems became available in this decade as both software and hardware capabilities improved. The application of these expert systems improved the productivity of processing more books, conducting more searches and serving more users each day. With the dawn of new millennium, Integrated Library Management Systems (ILMS) offered user friendly Graphical User Interface (GUI), and through hypertext technology, users are referred to other resources like electronic journals and other full text materials from in-house bibliographic or online public access catalogue records (Intuitive Products International, 2011).

Now-a-days, most of the major academic, special and public libraries of the world have installed integrated systems or are planning to procure and implement such systems to help librarians in providing effective access to information resources held within the library or elsewhere. Technological developments will perhaps continue to open new opportunities for libraries to provide efficient, exhaustive and expeditious information services and to link them worldwide irrespective of any barrier (Lynch, 1991). Though, it is said that technology has empowered libraries and has achieved all time success in improving their operations and functions for the sole purpose of better information delivery to users. But at the same time, librarians need to be self sufficient and techno competent to face the challenges that technology will bring with itself to the working environment of libraries and its staff.

INTERNATIONAL SCENARIO

Library technology like other fields, witnessed the supremacy of United States followed by United Kingdom. Though the lineage of term 'library automation' is traced back to 1930s, when punch cards developed by 'Hollerith' were first used in acquisition and circulation systems, but in actual practice, computer application begun to use in libraries in 1960s. The application of computers ushered American and British libraries in the era of computerization. With the result, different techniques were introduced during mid 20th century for streamlining circulation system, but the efforts taken during this century were by and large revolving around improving the manual system. However, some attempts were aimed to introduce mechanization to reduce the work of charging system (Martin, 1949). Further, Texas University used photo charging system by making use of punch cards and Unit Record System of IBM which focused on machine readable data.

During the subsequent quarter century, a number of other libraries incorporated IBM's Unit Record System into their circulation procedures. In this regard, IBM's Montclair system which resulted in most sophisticated automated circulation system in pre computer era was an outstanding exception. But despite its proven success, the use of automated circulation, because of its non-cost effectiveness never reached great extent in libraries. Till 1950s, the practice of automation in terms of machine readable records had not became widespread, as they were in limited use in circulation section. However, their use in Illinois Public Library made greater impact on acquisition section. The interest of computer application in libraries surfaced during 1950s and reached to a broader level in 1960s. Later in this decade, computer application introduced off line batch processing in libraries to enhance acquisition; cataloguing; circulation and serial control sections. By the mid 60s, more than 80 American academic libraries which shortly extended to 150 libraries, computerized their circulation system. Similarly, acquisition section was also computerized. During early 60s, several libraries like University of California and San Diego attempted to go beyond the listing of serials by implementing procedures for check-in and clearing (Salmon, 1969). One of the most important landmarks of this decade was the evolution of Library of Congress MARC format.

The decreasing size and price of computers lead to the development of mini- computers. The emergence of mini computers ushered libraries in the era of online automation as discussed earlier. Between late 60s and 70s, three trends like in-house projects, 'bibliographic utilities' and pre packaged 'Turnkey' automated systems evolved in the development of online library system. The first of such system was Illinois State Library System. In 1967, Midwestern University in Wichita Falls Texas implemented online circulation system and in 1968, the Booth Library at Eastern Illinois University in Charleston operated its own version of online circulation system. In the same year, Washington State University (WSU) library designed acquisition system, while university of Laval in Quebec set up online serials control system. By the decade of 70s, a number of academic libraries begun to incorporate mini computers in their circulation operations. The outstanding example was that of Ohio State University that facilitated users to search the item by call numbers, title key and a combination of author title key (Reynolds, 1985).

There were other large research libraries interested in online integrated system during this period, but actual implementation could be done only after several years of proper design, careful planning and experimentation. The

North-western Online Total Integrated System (NOTIS), the Chicago Library Data Management System and Stanford University's Bibliographic Automation of Large Library Operations (BALLOTS) were three famous large scale efforts of this time. The impact of BALLOTS, because of its adoption of RLG on American librarianship during 70s and 80s has been greater than any other system (Wayne, 1974). By the mid 70s, automated efforts in technical processing turned to shared systems. BALLOTS remained exemplary illustration of in-house system and became basis of networking system first among California libraries and then to wider area of Western America (Fayllot, 1972). The evolution of OCLC, RLG, WLN and UTLAS in 1967 extended their use by early 80s to several thousand North American libraries. Although, some libraries continued to develop their own in-house system for certain library functions, it was apparent by mid 70s that automated cataloguing was evolved in different directions and basis of this transportation was OCLC. Though in 1971 OCLC went online, but during its first year of online operation, it remained a cooperative venture of Ohio academic libraries, however, within four years, the usage of OCLC increased to 800 libraries (Research Libraries Group, 1978).

INDIGENOUS SCENARIO

After realizing the importance of computers for the progress and development of libraries in developed countries, a number of developing countries started on the same pattern and subsequently efforts were made at broader level for implementation of Information Technology (IT) in libraries.

In this regard, Indian Statistical Institute (ISI), Calcutta was the first to install computer system in 1955, but as far as application of computers in Indian libraries is concerned, Indian National Scientific and Documentation Centre (INSDOC) now NISCAIR (National

Institute of Science Communication and Information Resource) was possibly the first to computerize author and subject indexes of Indian Science Abstract (ISA) in 1965. However in 1967, INSDOC brought out roster of 'Indian Scientific and Technical Translators' with the help of computers. In 1973, INSDOC with the help of computers brought out first union catalogue by the name of "regional union catalogue of scientific serials" Bombay-Poona. In 1978, it initiated SDI service as a National Information System for Science and Technology (NISSAT) project with chemical abstracts and INSPEC databases with the use of CAN/SDI software of Indian Institute of Technology (IIT) Madras. In 1970s, a number of libraries ventured in preparing computerized databases. Through the initiative and financial assistance of NISSAT, many library networks like: CALIBNET; DELNET; INFLIBNET; PUNNET; NICNET; INDONET and SIRNET were notable networks that became operational (Sharma, 1995). Owing to the mass emergence of a number of library softwares and library networks across the country, the period of 1990s is popularly regarded as golden period in the history of library automation and networking in India.

There have been several organization and agencies which have pooled their efforts for automating Indian libraries and information centres at length and breadth. The notable of these organizations include:

- INSDOC Modern NISCAIR
- DRTC (Documentation Research Training Centre) at Bangalore
- DRDO (Defence Research Development Organization) at New Delhi
- DESIDOC (Defence Scientific Information and Documentation Centre) at New Delhi
- IISC (Indian Institute of Science) at Bangalore
- IIT Kanpur

- IIT Madras
- NIC (National Informatics Centre) AT New Delhi
- TIFR (Tate Institute of Fundamental Research) at Mumbai
- BARC (Baba Atomic Research Centre) at Mumbai
- PRL (Physical Research Laboratory) at Ahmadabad
- IGCARK (Indira Gandhi Centre for Atomic Research Kalpakam) at Chennai
- NISSAT (National Information System in Science and Technology)
- DELNET (Developing Library Network) at New Delhi
- RRFL (Raja Ram Mohan Roy Library Foundation)
- INFLIBNET (Information and Library Network), at Ahmadabad, Gujarat
- UGC (University Grants Commission) at New Delhi

It is notable to mention here that some of these organizations and agencies periodically conduct extensive training programs for Indian and SAARC librarians for automating the college and university libraries in India and abroad. The librarians and other library and information professionals from all corners of the country enthusiastically participate in these detailed training courses on library automation. Some organizations particularly NISCAIR, DRTC, IISC, INFLIBNET, DELNET and DESIDOC also conduct some courses on library automation with detailed hands on training to a number of library software packages popularly used in Indian libraries. Of these organizations, some have also developed indigenous library software packages for automating Indian libraries and information centres. The notable softwares packages developed by some of these organizations include SOUL (Software for University Libraries) developed by INFLIBNET, Granthalaya software package developed by NISCAIR, DELMS library package developed by DESIDOC, Sanjay software package also developed by DESIDOC, iit-KLAS (Kanpur Library Automation Software) etc. However, most of the packages developed by these organizations could not survive long owing to their shortcomings in compatibility with international standards. All these library software packages have been discussed in detail in chapter-3 of this book. Some of these organizations also run courses like PGDLAN (Post Graduate Diploma in Library Automation and Networking) which has proved very successful in enhancing the technical skill of Indian library and information science professionals. Owing majorly to incompatibility issues of Indian library software packages with international standards, many large and reputed Indian libraries have/are switching over to standard foreign library management packages such as Virtua, Alice for Windows, etc. for automating their library system to effectively stay vibrant in the present world of techno savvy users.

In addition to above, many institutions are engaged in imparting training for application of computers in library work through number of sponsored, ad hoc and regular refresher courses. This introduction of IT followed by the new emerging technologies and falling price of computer hardware and software, special libraries attached with Research and Development (R&D) organizations along with college and university libraries attained prominent place in the country. Despite of the fact that progress towards automation in India initially received Luke warm response, but with the adequate grants from University Grants Commission (UGC) and respective State Governments, the number of academic, special and public libraries to automate their operations and services have been increased manifold (Sharma, 1995).

AUTOMATION AND RESOURCE SHARING

Though resource sharing/library cooperation existed even

centuries before when Alexandra library shared its resources with Pergamon library. However in 1974, Research Libraries Group (RLG) comprising Harvard; Yale; Columbia and New York Public Library was set up with the primary objective of actual and effective resource sharing, collection development and preservation and conservation of library materials. During the decade of 70s, Washington State Library designed an online bibliographic system which went online in 1977. By 1978, the Washington Library Network was used in 12 public and 9 academic libraries in the State and 2 other libraries in Alaska, while 3 libraries in Idaho and 1 in Oregon later joined WLN (WLN Reports, 1979). In the same year, University of Toronto Library Automation System (UTLAS) was established in Canada, but its impact on United States has been limited. By the end of the decade, UTLAS increased its membership to 200 libraries and later extended to US and Japan.

Though WLN, OCLC and RLIN made tremendous impact on American librarianship during the decade of 70s in providing online cataloguing, but their impact on circulation, acquisition and serials check-in was negligible (Reynolds, 1985). However, commercial vendors of automated library system in the area of online circulation handled other technical processing. In this regard, Computer Library System Inc. (now CLSI) at Cleveland Public Library in 1972 was the early commercial vendor. The first effort involved acquisition system, but soon it turned attention to circulation with the development of LIBIS 100 system which came to be known as "Turnkey system". By 1975, five commercial vendors were offering Turnkey automated circulation; however in 1977, several new vendors like DataPhase, Geac and Universal library system entered the market. But, CLSI was more powerful with 177 installations and more than 300 other libraries using it. The fastest growing competitor was Data Phase with 50 installations followed by Geac with 22 and Gaylord (active since 1978) had 11 installations by 1981. In 1977, the Plessey Online Circulation System became popular in Great Britain and had 9 users in USA and Canada (C. L. Systems, 1981).

The early 80s represented an intense period in the development of online catalogue. However since mid 80s, online catalogue implementation have been dominated by Integrated Library Systems (ILS) which combine database management and catalogue access capabilities with circulation control, acquisition, serials control and other operations. Such systems may be implemented as complete turnkey configuration of hardware and software or as prewritten software packages designed to operate on library-owned mainframe, mini-computer or micro computer. Vendors in this direction include CLSI; Geac; NOTIS; Dynix; OCLC; Virginia Tech; Data Research Associates; Carlyle; Comstow Information Systems; Universal Library Systems; George Town Medical Library; Washington University; IBM; Sirsi; UTLAS and many more recently designed systems have been active in marketing and promoting library automation. The newest and most widely publicized approaches to online catalogue implementation were the growing number of vendors offering Public Access catalogue systems on CD-ROMS (Saffady, 1989).

As more libraries obtained online catalogue, retrospective conversion of bibliographic records gained interest. Thus, many retrospective conversion projects in 1980s resulted in explosion of MARC records in union catalogues like OCLC and RLG. Also in the 1980s, MARC broke out of the ASCII and extended Latin character sets when one of the major networks, RLG, developed standard character sets for many languages. During 1990s, MARC format evolved in reaction to the exciting possibilities of internet technology. This format addressed several major issues including the need to provide linking to actual resources from bibliographic record. An additional development in this period has been an attempt to separate MARC data elements from MARC structure (ISO 2709) to represent highly developed MARC data elements in Standard Generalized Markup Language (SGML) or Extensible Mark Language (XML). Further in 1990s, the availability of systems that fundamentally support MARC 21, and the MARC 21 orientation of several of the large record repositories like OCLC, have been an incentive for countries to rethink and realign this format with MARC 21. This globalization of original MARC format has moved the international MARC community towards a new level of consistency through standardization of content designation that was not possible earlier. The complete alignment of MARC format used in US with CAN/MARC from Canada in 1997 has been beneficial to North American libraries that already corporate in many ways. The decision of British Library in 2001 to cease the maintenance of United Kingdom Machine Readable Catalogue Records (UKMARC) in favor to MARC 21 also had major impact on global MARC standardization for library automation (McCallum, 2002).

Recently, the application of expert systems made a great impact on library activities such as reference services, indexing, cataloguing, Decision Support System and front-end systems for database searching. These expert systems serve more patrons, especially at peak hours resulting in more user satisfaction without having to hire more reference librarians. With the development of more advanced silicon computer chips; enlarged storage capacity; faster access; ever improved telecommunication links and ability to quickly process, store, disseminate and retrieve information, the current information delivery services have flourished to a great extent (Aluri & Riggs, 1988). All these developments played a key role in automating American and British libraries. Pertinently, these developments shall serve as a road map to automate the libraries for effective resource sharing to avoid cost implications which is the major bottleneck for automating the libraries of developing countries including India. The development of American and British librarianship for the successful automated library system shall serve as an eye opener for developing economies for automating their libraries on the same lines.

REFERENCES

Aluri, R., & Riggs, D. E. (1988). Application of Expert System to Libraries. In Joe A. Hewitt (Ed.)., *Advances in Library Automation and Networking* (Vol. 2, pp. 8-9) London: JAI Press.

Aswal, R. S. (2006). *Library Automation for 21st Century.* New Delhi: ESS ESS, pp. 56-57.

Bajirjian, R. (1995). *New Automation Technology for Acquisitions and Collection Development.* New York: The Haworth Press, p. 5.

Cohn, J., Ann, M., Kelsey, L., & Fiels, K. M. (2002). *Planning for Integrated Systems and Technologies: A how-to-do-it Manual for Libraries.* London: Facet, xviii.

C. L. Systems. (1981). C. L. Systems Holds Commanding Lead among Circulation Systems Marketers. *Advanced Technology Libraries,* 10, 1-7.

Dutta, N. (1993). *The Use of PC's in Library Automation; Information Technology & Health Science Libraries.* New Delhi: Medical Library Association of India, pp. 59-66.

Fayllot, J. (1972). Online Serials Control System in a Large Biomedical Library. *Journal for American Society for Information Science,* 318-322.

Feather, J., & Sturges, R. P. (2003). Library automation. In *International Encyclopedia of Information and Library Science* (p. 377). London: Roultledge.

Halsey, W. D. (1987). Library automation. In *Collier's Encyclopedia* (Vol. 3, p. 326). New York: Macmillan.

Head, J. W., & McCabe, G. B. (1996). *Introducing and Managing Academic Library Automation Projects.* Westport: Greenwood, p. 3.

Heiliger, E. M., & Paul, B. H. (1970). *Library Information Systems:*

From Library Automation to Distributed Information Access Solutions. Westport: Libraries Unlimited, p. 333.

Intuitive Products International. (2011). *A Brief History of Library Automation; Research Papers.* Retrieved January 20, 2010 from http://www.Justfreepapers.com/papers/15926/abriefhistoryoflibraryaut

Johnson, E. D. (1965). *A History of Libraries in the Western World.* New York: The Scare Crow, pp. 7-8.

Keefer, A., & Baiget, T. (2001). How it all Began: A Brief History of the Internet. *Vine,* 31(3), 90-91. DOI: 10.1108/03055720010804221

Kothari, C. R. (2004). *Research Methodology Methods and Techniques.* New Delhi: New Age International, pp. 184-185.

Lynch, C. A. (1991). The System Perspective. In Gary M. Pitkin (Ed.)., *The Evolution of Library Automation Management Issues and Future Perspectives* (p. 39). Westport: Meckler.

Martin, A. B. (1949). Tulsa Finds New Aid in Photographic Charging. *Library Journal,* 74, 1476.

McCallum, S. H. (2002). MARC: Keystone for Library Automation. *IEEE Annals of the History of Computing,* Library of Congress, 45-47. Retrieved Feb 23, 2010 from http://www.ieeexplore.ieee.org/iels

Research Libraries Group (1978). Research Libraries Group goes for BALLOTS. *Library Journal,* 103, 916.

Reynolds, D. (1985). *Library Automation Issues and Applications.* New York: R. R. Bowker, pp. 41-63.

Reitz, J. M. (2004). *Dictionary of Library and Information Science.* Westport: Libraries Unlimited.

Riaz, M. (1992). *Library Automation.* New Delhi: Atlantic, p. 61.

Riggs, D. E. (1992). The Library Perspective. In Gary M. Pitkin (Ed.)., *The Evolution of Library Automation Management Issues and Future Perspectives* (p. 20). Westport: Meckler.

Saffady, W. (1989). Library Automation: An Overview. *Library Trends,* 37(3), 273-277.

Savage, C. M. (1996). *Fifth Generation Management: Co-creating through Virtual Enterprising, Dynamic Teaming, and Knowledge Networking.* (Rev. 2nd ed., p. 176). Woburn: Butterworth-Heinemann. Retrieved May 8, 2010 from http://Books.google.co.in/books?id

Salmon, S. R. (Ed.). (1969). *Library Automation: A State of Art Review.* Chicago: American Library Association, p. 139.

Sharma, P. S. K. (1995). *Fundamentals of Library Automation with Illustrations.* New Delhi: ESS ESS, pp. 113-114.

Swihart, S., & Hefley, B. F. (1973). *Computer Systems in the Library: a Handbook for Managers & Designers.* California: Melville, pp. 11-271.

The New Encyclopedia Britannica (1973). Automation. In *Macropedia* (Vol. 14, p. 548). Chicago: Encyclopedia Britannica.

The New Oxford American Dictionary (2001). Oxford: Oxford University Press, p. 109.

Tyre, L. (1995). Library Automation; it is all about Connections. *Technological Horizons in Education,* 23(3), 60. Retrieved July 17, 2009 from http://www.questia.com/read

Voight, M. J. (1956). The Trend Toward Mechanization in Libraries. University of Illinois at Urbana-Champaign: Graduate School of Library and Information Science. *Library Trends,* 5 (2), 193-205.

Wallace, D. P., & Joan, G. (1989) Microcomputers in Libraries. *Library Trends,* 37(4), 288-289.

Wayne, D. (1972). *Mini computers and Library Automation; the Standard Experience: Proceedings of the 1974 Clinic on Library Applications and Data Processing.* Urbana, III: University of Illinois Graduate School of Library Science, 87-89.

Webb, T. D. (1987). *The in-House option: Professional Issues of Library Automation.* New York: The Haworth Press, pp. vii-viii.

Wedgeworth, R. (1993). Library automation. In *World Encyclopedia of Library and Information Services* (pp. 470-471). Michigan: American Library Association.

WLN Reports. (1979). WLN Reports Beachhead Down Under. *LJ/LSJ Hotline,* 8(4), 2.

Young, H. (Ed.). (1983). *The ALA Glossary of Library & Information Science.* Chicago: ALA, p. 18.

2

Planning for Library Automation

This chapter discusses about the different steps involved in planning a thoughtful library automation project. All the steps have been elaborated one by one with some examples for their fuller and better understanding. It also broadly discusses about the hardware and other software requirements for implementing a successful automation project in college and university libraries of India.

BACKGROUND

The term library automation simply refers to the application of computers and other mechanized and semiautomatic equipment in performing various routine housekeeping activities of libraries in a better way for the benefit of their end users. This application of computers in libraries has relieved librarians from many routine, administrative and other clerical activities. However, automation cannot completely replace the librarian or his involvement in taking any decision regarding the professional judgement of the libraries. There would always be the requirement of skilful cataloguers and classifiers for cataloguing and classification activities in any kind of libraries, whatsoever would be the infrastructure available. Moreover, public contacts of libraries also cannot be automated; therefore, the librarian touch will remain even in fully automated library system.

PLANNING FOR AUTOMATING LIBRARIES

In planning library automation project, there would be many premier factors which will call for prior considerations before taking up the project. Of these factors, some of the important ones according to Swihart and Hefly (1973) are enumerated here under one by one:

1. Clarifying the Objectives of Automation
2. Administrative approval of the Project
3. What needs to be Done?
4. Sequential Implementation
5. Project should not get out of Hands
6. Who shall be involved in the Implementation of the Project?
7. Sequence of Applications in the Automation Project
8. Involvement of Human Factors

All these prior considerations of library automation project are discussed one by one in detail hereunder:

1. CLARIFYING THE OBJECTIVES OF AUTOMATION

The first and foremost objective of any library automation project should be based on the fact that what library actually wishes to accomplish by automating. It should include the priorities like purpose and scope of the project. It should not forget to frame a timeline for the completion of the project, besides being cautious to prescribe the limits of the project. Librarian should not also forget to assign a specific person, who besides skilful, may be capable professional for the development part of the project.

Since university and college libraries are a large setup and there would be many professionals looking after the different library activities, therefore, it would be feasible for the Head Librarian to call upon the subordinate librarians for chalking out the objectives that demands first attention in the project. He may also go on to chalk out what is feasible to accomplish and in what time scale. But for this purpose, librarian has to be a skilful manager to take these management decisions. Library management shall not only go ahead for the project for the sake of Machine against Man. However, the project shall be handled in such a way that both machine and man suit the library requirements in more effective and efficient way than ever before.

In this direction, librarian should define some objectives that are to be solved by automating the library system. In other words, it can be stated that a draft of requirements shall be designed in such a way that it can cover most of the requirements including scope and purpose of a particular library. In this case, librarian can ask for help from system analyst to prepare a well thought out draft of requirements. Further, if it is a standalone automation which is a gone by idea in modern era, then librarian should prioritize the parts or operations having most benefits in less investment. However, in case of integrated library management systems, all operations can be automated at one time. Swihart and Hefley in their work have designed following requirements/objectives that a library may expect from automating:

- Computers shall provide the librarians and users with more information faster than with the manual methods and visible records.
- They should be easy to use for librarians and users without requiring extensive training.
- Computer enabled library activities shall also be less costly than manually done activities.
- All operations which can be automated shall be serviceable.
- Computerized activities shall be flexible and

modular without substantial redesigning.

- Updation of records shall be simple
- Data exchange/resource sharing with other libraries is an important function of libraries; it should be capable to do it.
- Should be capable of operating in both centralization and decentralization modes.
- Shall not be burdened with unusual and huge machinery which may create space issues.

2. ADMINISTRATIVE APPROVAL OF THE PROJECT

The head librarian along with his most capable professionals with a good computer knowledge background shall chalk out the design errors, misunderstandings, omissions, or any other issues, if any in the previously framed requirement cum objective draft. Here modifications for further improvement may be incorporated, in case the policy is to be revisited. The managerial skill of the librarian and the designing ability of system analyst would be more demanding here to consider all these points. The draft of requirements may be needed to be redrafted, before a consensus among head librarian and his capable professionals reach to a conclusion on some definite objectives and better interior designing of the entire automation project. Once the head librarian and his key colleagues sense a full satisfaction of drafted objectives of the automation project, the draft will be sent to the higher ups or top management of the university/college for its administrative approval.

In case, the project happened to be small which is not normally the case with university/college library automation, the project can be get approved at lower level with small modification, if found necessary. However, for the automation of college and university libraries, the drafted proposal may be required to be studied for further feasibility and specifications. This kind of draft is normally appropriate for top level approval. This proposal should markedly indicate the guidelines, finance, performance, services and standards in such a fashion that non-library people may also understand it quickly for uneventful approval. It will, however, be more appropriate to have a live demonstration of such a proposal before the top authorities both at university and at INFLIBNET and UGC level which are main funding agencies of automating college and university libraries in India. Notably, the demonstration will clear doubted minds which may hamper the project. It is pertinent to point out here that presently there are a number of automation project designs available on internet with better interior designing facilities.

Once approved by the top management, the automation project will also require continuous financial cooperation and coordination for annual maintenance charges from the authorities for its effective implementation.

3. WHAT NEEDS TO BE DONE?

The first consideration in what needs to be done shall be to develop specifications.

Specifications

The librarian should establish in detail the specifications which thereafter shall establish what requirements are to be accomplished by the automation project. In developing these specifications, specific methods of how these objectives are accomplished shall be framed out. However, if there are certain known technologies as is the case with integrated library management systems, for accomplishing the objectives, then it is suggested to omit the specific methods. In case the technologies and other methods are not available, then the designed specifications' may be justifiable. Nevertheless, such specifications can only be developed after a thorough system study reassessing all the library operations within the scope of the drafted proposal. The proposal must be inclusive and examined in detail what to do so that during the design stage, issues over the feasibility of some other services may not arise. It can also over burden the project with financial implications than anticipated in the first proposal.

In case of large library automation project, it may be divided into phase wise with each phase separately installed. Though detailed specifications would be developed for one phase at one point of time, however, general specifications for all phases should be developed as a single unit. Care shall also be taken that project should not go out hands. If each phase is developed separately at different times, the later phases are most likely incompatible with the earlier phases. The librarian shall ensure that the project shall be handled in such a way that wasting time, money and effort be avoided at every cost.

Designing the System

This is the phase of accomplishing "how to do" the "what to do" framed in the general specifications. According to Swihart, a system design shall include layouts, input formats, file structures and contents, work flow, balancing, audit and edit controls, production schedules, etc. The librarian in thoughtful consultation with the system analyst shall prepare the design report in a very non-technical terminology for its better understanding and installation.

Feasibility Study

A system is always feasible, if it performs the desired functions in a desired time at a rational price within the scope of accomplishing drafted objectives of the organization or a library. In a non-profit organization like library, costs however, may exceed in accomplishing the objectives. But this won't go well with the profit making organizations. In case the system doesn't meet the desired standards, then there is likely chance of its being not feasible. It is always suggested that no system should either be accepted to management for approval nor should it be approved by the management without prior feasibility study. However, it may not be also appropriate to consider every minor issue which can be solved easily at local level in a system. But, the system installed with modest study may also turn otherwise to operate as per the plan. Normally the system should comprise following for feasibility:

- Total number of users to be added in the system
- Cost of the automated operations shall be included
- Cost of system analysis, design and feasibility studies
- Cost of manual work to be left
- Overhead costs
- Intangible costs
- Costs of inability to perform some necessary functions, and
- Time period for implementation

It is also advised that the costs of designing and implementing the system shall also be worked out and kept separate from operational costs.

Final Management Approval

Besides getting the project approved from the top administrative level, the large library automation projects may be asked for management approval, before implementation. After the system design and feasibility study, the librarian may have to present the management with documented facts instead of virtual benefits. In case the presentation of facts was found accurate, there would be no further approval required and the system design will be final. However, if bigger differences were smelled, management would have second thoughts for the approval of the project. While in smaller differences, the project normally gets approved with minor suggestions (Moore, 1967).

4. SEQUENTIAL IMPLEMENTATION

As long as the project is approved by the top level authorities, the next course of action would be to design the desired computer programs for the implementation of the project. These computer programs will further be required for assigning the coding. Each computer program should be tested separately with some theoretical or sometimes practical library data. This shall be followed by the testing of all the separately tested data in a complete dummy operation to check out the fitting output of everything in the system. This dummy operation would be very fruitful in identifying the errors, omissions and other issues, if any, which were not considered when testing on individual computer program was made. It, thereby, screens the complete operation of the system and eradicates the inefficiencies, if any.

Training of Library Professionals

The designing the computer programs would be followed by the training of library professionals. Every library professional whose assigned library operation affects the newly placed system would be required to go for the training which shall be of different types like clerical librarians, professional cataloguers and computer operators, etc. Training should be as extensive as possible. There are many agencies including INFLIBNET, NISCAIR, DESIDOC, DRTC, ISI, etc. as stated earlier, which periodically conduct some training programs for the automating college and university libraries in India.

Pilot Project

For large library automation projects, a pilot project is

always advisable before implementing the system fully. It may be mentioned here that the pilot project implies on a small proportion of the actual data or operations to be processed through a new system of working. The pilot project also establishes the fact that the new system is operating satisfactorily.

Revisions

In this phase, the project is revised for incorporating modifications and other suggestions worked out in pilot project for obtaining the maximum benefits out of the system. Sometimes the reports which in the design stage appeared good in one order may now in actual operation appear best sorted in another order. It is suggested that the same people should participate in the revision phase who actually took part in the development of specifications and designing the system for planning changes, if any, to ensure that the changes or modifications are carried out correctly.

Installation

Once the system has worked unchanged for some time, the library can begin the installation of other phases. During the earlier times of automation, libraries were required to install the projects in a phased manner. However, in the present context of integrated library management systems, libraries can completely install the entire automation project at onetime, after its successful pilot study phase.

5. PROJECT SHOULD NOT GET OUT OF HANDS

Direction

In order to avoid that the automation project does not get out of control, the university librarian in case of universities shall assign one of the senior and most skilful professional to be in charge of the project. This skilful professional should be able to devote as much time as required for the project. However, he/she should be relaxed from his/her other official engagements either fully or partially till the completion of the project. Sometimes a fairly good project turns poorly designed, in case a dedicated professional is not assigned as the in charge of the project for its proper supervision.

Compatibility with Specifications

In order that the system analysts and computer programmers may not deviate from the original specifications which have been thoroughly worked out during the different previous phases, the project leader or simply the assigned skilful professional shall be given written instructions and specifications for controlling conformity. In some cases, some libraries strictly direct the system analysts and programmers to follow the designed specifications for the conformity, even though system analysts and computer programmers may be right in making to look the system simpler. However, the project library leader may think of changes during the implementation phase for the improvement in results. These changes are liable to be incorporated and tested only after proper approval.

Cost and Schedule Limits

The costs and schedule limits in computer oriented projects are often exceeded. In this direction Swihart and Hefly have suggested several following reasons:

- Some organizations do not plan the project well in advance in thorough detail to be aware of just how much work is required to get the system installed.
- Changes are often desired during the implementation phase.
- Library projects are above all other projects, and, are therefore, subject to estimating errors.
- Lax project supervision is also a factor.

The automation project is possible to be controlled by establishing the size of the project and the cost before beginning for implementation. Afterwards at periodical intervals, by comparing the time estimates with the amount of work already accomplished. This can identify the delays and causes are studied for their correctness. It may be pointed out here that controlling the project is difficult without an adequate implementation plan.

System Documentation

Once the system is in operation, an up-to-date documentation should be brought out. Generally, a good documentation comprises the following:

- A general level description of the application. This is mostly the same proposal submitted to management for approval.
- Detail level procedures, this should comprise the clerical procedures used in the library.
- File structure and records, this comprises the complete description of contents of each file, their sequence and methods of verifying the validity of entered data.
- Disaster protection, this shall include the description of duplication files and their maintenance in the library.

6. WHO SHALL BE INVOLVED IN THE IMPLEMENTATION OF THE PROJECT?

This important phase of automation project details about those persons who shall participate in the implementation of their automation project. In case of smallest libraries with few library staff, librarian can persuade every other personnel for implementation of the project. But for large university and college level library automation project, following personals would be required for implementing the project:

Manager

Being the non-profit service oriented institution; university libraries would require the high level management for successful implementation. This library manager would also get in touch with the library staff to develop them towards the change that the new system will bring with itself.

Librarian

Librarian would be the most important person involved in implementation. He would actually ensure that whether all the interests of users of library, library functions and services to be automated are taken into consideration or not. He would also ensure which operation and services are to be given priority in automating. However in the present world of standard library management systems, all operations and services are automated at onetime with much ease as compared to the earlier days of automation.

Project Leader

The project leader has been in the supervision of all phases of the project and obviously has developed a good knowledge about the project. Therefore, he/she may fulfil his function of supervision for the implementation as he/she stimulates, controls and seeks better ways to do the things for encouraging the improvements in service with reduction in costs.

Content Specialists

The content specialist in case of libraries is mostly the person who is well versed with the library collection and its materials. This person may be less technical for the implementation participation, but his involvement for what needs to be accomplished to provide the satisfactory services is essential, since he/she possesses mastery over the collection of the library. He/she possess different level of proficiency, since being familiar with the issues related with different subjects' collection of the library.

Technique Specialists

This skilful person would possess experience in analysing and designing the procedures for accomplishing the work more effectively. He/she is known of equipments, methods, technical procedures, machinery, technological tools, modern gadgets and strategy for combining all these or some of these to get the desired results with minimum effort and cost. It is also suggested that such kind of persons also have some mastery over handling subject matter during implementation phase. These persons can design the system to handle the needs of a library from their skills gained from automating different libraries in case of external implementation and listening to content specialists and general knowledge of problem solving techniques and data handling techniques, etc.

Programmers

These are the people mostly related with computer programming who can program or set up other procedures for computer systems, printing devices, microfilm readers, and key punching, etc. They read specifications made by the technique specialists and write programs and develop procedures. These programmers test situations to authenticate that their programs are run properly and correctly for installation.

In-House or External Implementation

Normally, there are four types which can be considered in implementing library automation projects. These are discussed hereunder:

- Local library project or implementing the project within the library.
- External agencies of some system/computing organization implementing the project.
- A contract between the library and some consulting house usually the vendors of library management packages for implementing the project.

- A combination of all of the above

Each of the above types has their own pros and cons. However, when the project is awarded to some reputed external organization, the benefits are usually of high standards, because of their qualitative workmanship owing to their experience in installing the project in a number of libraries. In the context of present integrated library management systems, the vendors of all standard packages have a high level experienced group of professionals who implement the automation project within the stipulated schedule and cost. In comparison, if the project is taken up for implementation at local level, it is less likely to be finished within the set timeline and the set budget. Moreover, the lack of expertise at local level often turns the project into poorly designed and poorly implemented.

7. SEQUENCE OF APPLICATIONS IN THE AUTOMATION PROJECT

Every library has their requirement and heterogeneous users. Therefore, it won't be fruitful to recommend a particular sequence of application to all the libraries. A skilful librarian will always take into consideration his/her library requirements and heterogeneous nature of users prior to choosing some specific sequence of applications for implementation of the automation project. However, there are some common internal factors which power the selection of sequence in converting the different library operations to machine operations. Nonetheless, the most advisable and preferred sequence of library operations for implementation of automation would include:

- Acquisition
- Cataloguing
- Circulation
- Serials control

- OPAC and
- Information retrieval

All these operations are discussed in the following paras.

Acquisition

Acquisition would logically be the first operation of library to call for automation, since every other activity happens after acquisition. To automate a library, acquisition operation should always be the first choice. In this operation, new titles are ordered and duplicate checking is carried out. All this is possible to be accomplished with much ease in an automated acquisition system. There is requirement for selected materials to be checked in pre-order, on-order, in process and already catalogued materials. These necessities are better handled independently in automated acquisition system. Acquisition forms the core activity in any library which requires sound knowledge of librarianship. It is rightly said that once the automation of acquisition is done effectively, the whole of library automation project would be effective, since acquisition is considered as the starting point of library automation project. In traditional acquisition, problems in monitoring mounting collections, preparing and updating supplier list, sending reminders and management of budget were a common issues. However, modern libraries founded a total solution to these troubles in an automated acquisition system. It is a common perception that librarians had never imagined that their task would be so simple with the help of library automation software (Rajgopalan, 1981).

The automation of acquisition system of libraries has been discussed in detail in chapter-4.

Cataloguing

After acquisition, the responsibility directly shifts on the cataloguers to keep the collection ready for circulation for its ultimate use. In a manual library, cataloguers had to tackle a lot of issues in the cataloguing process, majorly due of lacking of standardization. It may be stated here that one of the wonderful benefits of automating cataloguing is the standardization. The acquisition shall follow by automation of cataloguing section in the libraries. There are several steps involved in the process of cataloguing. These steps are:

- Cataloguing standards
- Entry in the machine readable form (MARC Based entry)
- Production of catalogue cards
- Reconcile the conflicting file data

Prior to the processing of any cataloguing data in the computer, there has to be a very careful framework on what information is to be entered in the computer based catalogue. It is also to be agreed upon the fact that in what manner these computer based catalogues are to be maintained. For this purpose, there are certain global cataloguing standards of uniformity which must be followed, before starting the automation of cataloguing. These standards are discussed in the cataloguing module of chapter-4.

After following these standards in cataloguing, the next course of action would be to enter the cataloguing records in machine readable form or simply the data should be entered in MARC based entry. This process may involve the copying of cataloguing data from catalogue cards onto magnetic tapes or disks.

The next step would be the production of catalogue cards either in book format or in the catalogue cards. The last step is to resolve the difference, if any, between the earlier forms of cataloguing and to resolve the faults in copying from traditional catalogue to computer catalogue. The automation of cataloguing can better be understood from cataloguing module elaborated in chapter-4.

Circulation

Circulation control was regarded as one of the first major operations of automated libraries during 1960s in the western world (Haravu, 2004). It was perhaps the primary operation which got a lot of consideration at global level. One finds it right to say that the efficiency of entire automation project lies in the effectiveness of its circulation control. It is one of the technological operations of the library where a user directly contacts with the library system. In traditional prolonged and time consuming circulation, users had to waste much of their valuable time in standing at queues at circulation counter for their requested resources. However in modern automated circulation, borrowers are now issuing and returning library materials themselves on self check-in and check-out stations. This modern automated circulation system has greatly increased the users' believability in the retrieval system of modern libraries. The introduction of bar-coding also overthrew the burden of manual labour intensive circulation exercise to a great deal. Further the prompt reminders via e-mail about the due date and fines levelled against the late returns have also eased the pressure on traditional manual stamping of due date slips and fault prone calculation of fines. Apart from reducing the stretched lines at circulation counter, automated circulation has proved very successful in having greater control over loaned items. Oyemakinde and Evans (1979) also approve this viewpoint.

If this circulation control is automated before the availability of catalogue in computer form, there will be a considerable file creation process, in some form, in order to get sufficient descriptive information on the items in circulation, and this catalogue file preparation may require major review, when, at later time, the decision is made to automate the cataloguing (Swihart and Hefly, 1973). For fuller and better understanding of automating circulation control, see full description of automation of circulation in chapter-4.

Serials Control

Automating Serials control is said to be as one of the most tedious library operations, there would not be many academic libraries in India which till date may have fully automated their serials control system. On the other hand, developing a serials control module is also considered a tedious job for library software developers, while installation and functioning of serials module is evenly difficult job for librarians. It will be no wonder to mention that software vendors of almost all integrated library management systems get the maximum complaints in connection with the operationalization of serials control module. It is mainly due to a number of idiosyncrasies concerned in the serials publications.

During the initial period of automation, the chief function of computers with relation to serials control was the updating and printing of serials list (Reynolds, 1985). Traditionally, the idea of using data processing techniques to serials publication started to draw consideration as before as 1949 when punch-cards were applied in serials procurement at the University of Texas Library (Steward, 1968). Afterwards during 1960s, many libraries in US tried to automate many procedures concerned with serials control. In this direction, University of California was first to do so.

The automation of serials control in Indian libraries particularly academic libraries has not taken off like other operations. In this case, it is recommended that the sequence to automate the serials control would be once all other operations are automated, since there is a big query of different tasks like binding and entering number of issues of a single volume of a journal in the database which normally does not take place in other operations. The automation of serials control has been given in elaboration in chapter-4 of this book. Since some standard library management softwares such as LibSys, Virtua and Alice for Windows, etc. also offer Article indexing module, however, this module has lost the relevance in the present world of World Wide Web where there are millions and billions of full text articles available on internet at affordable costs. It may also be mentioned here that many Indian university and college libraries subscribe many international full text databases for the benefit of their bonafide users. Hence, the article indexing module, though available in the library software package of many libraries is rarely being utilized in Indian libraries now-a-days. Nevertheless, its usage has been hailed in the earlier times of Indian library automation.

OPAC

The sequence of OPAC module in the implementation of automation project in libraries would be recommended at last, but one. It is in this important module of any library software package where users actually interact with a particular library's collection. The inception of standard integrated library management systems has shifted the mechanism of searching and retrieving information from manual to online methods. Remarkably, OPAC has been a significant development in this direction to help library borrowers to browse and trace their desired books within a blink by clicking the required push button on the keyboard. This OPAC has been debated and discussed in a detailed account in chapter-5 for the fuller and easier understanding.

Information Retrieval

The availability of enormous publications in the universe of knowledge has created some big challenges for librarians to provide the fast and accurate access to this literature. This literature explosion pushed the librarians to wall for automating their access and retrieval system as per the desired demand by the users. In any automated library system, its information access and retrieval system forms the key subsystem of whole automation project. It is not surprising to note that the retrieval system of a particular library is straightly linked to its users' satisfaction. Rather, the success of entire automation project lies in the effectiveness and efficiency of its information access and retrieval system.

Information retrieval activities constitute the following services:

- Current Awareness Service (CAS),
- Selective Dissemination of Information services (SDI),
- Automated reference services,
- Bibliographic services,
- Electronic Document Delivery Services (EDDS),
- Announcement bulletin, and
- Flash news, Display news, etc.

For the matter of the sequence of implementing automation project, the automation of these services should be implemented at end of the automation project, seen from the users' standpoint. These information retrieval services have been further discussed in detail in chapter-5.

8. INVOLVEMENT OF HUMAN FACTORS

The human factors involved in planning and implementing a good automation project in libraries have been discussed hereunder:

Steady Approach

Automating large university and college libraries is not an overnight job or magic wand to accomplish within the shortest time. The installation of an automated system will take its time. The library has to start form the conversion and retro conversion of records, which itself takes months together. However, in the present era of standard integrated library management systems, automating libraries has become though easier, but not possible within days. Nevertheless, in case of newly established libraries and small sized libraries, automating their operations would be easier and less time consuming, since they have to start all the processes afresh and there won't be any shifting or copying of data from one form to another. There won't also be the change in policies and standards on previously used styles.

It is difficult to forecast the problems that will arise in implementation and it is more important to set right the active system than to install the subsequent subsystem in the line. In this view, it is recommended that a gradualistic approach may be adopted in the implementation of the project.

Human Involvement

There are several considerations to be kept in mind during the different phases of development and implementation of automation project in the libraries. These considerations include:

- Resistance to change,
- Job permanence,
- Automation and computer techno fears,
- Apprehensions of errors in the new system, and
- Extensive training.

All these considerations are discussed one by one below.

Resistance to Change

Some people intentionally or unintentionally resist for changes that automation will bring with itself. They prefer to remain the traditional and won't accept the new systems fearing that they will be out thrown, because of their traditional approaches. These people are unmoved, even after explaining all the pros and cons, advantages and disadvantages and other benefits of implementing new automated library systems. The librarian should try best to motivate such persons and if they could not be persuaded, then the project should go ahead as per the plan, because their resistance won't do any good for the future of the library.

Job Permanence

Like other organizations, computers have proved boon for modernizing libraries and their operations to a great extent. They have reduced the manual effort involved in many operations of the libraries; however, they should not be deemed as complete replacement of machine against man. Some people including less skilled librarians have developed a kind of fear that computers may not eliminate their positions. These people in the technical terminology are called as techno fears. Nevertheless, the position of professional librarians will never be eliminated at the cost of computers. They will find their applications in all the professional operations of libraries till libraries exist. However, the stand of clerical people may have some apprehensions in fully automated library systems which shall be discussed prior to planning of automation project in the library. These clerical positions, however, can be assigned other computer related functions or can be transferred to their suited divisions in case of universities and colleges. Nonetheless, such complete automated library systems are yet to be fully operational in India.

Automation and Computer Techno Fears

The persons who possess less computer knowledge or are techno illiterates are always at the threat of being replaced by machines. These techno fears may be directed to visit other departments for computer training and an extensive tour of automated libraries of the same area or nearby states may eradicate their frightening with computers. The professional librarians with less or no computer knowledge may be made to undergo the training courses conducted in this direction by INFLIBNET, NISCAIR, DRDO, DESIDOC, DRTC, ISI, etc., in India. Pertinently, these organizations periodically conduct automation training programs for Indian and SAARC librarians.

Apprehensions of Errors

Indian librarians mostly fear of errors for implementing automated library systems. It has been seen that they rarely go for hit and trial method, barring some librarians at IIT Level. They also fear that if any complication aroused in the automation project, they may be taken to task by top management, though it has never happened in Indian university and college libraries. The use of trustworthy and skilled persons with sufficient testing techniques and training will, however, help Indian librarians in preventing such apprehensions of automation. Further, the application of standard and leading integrated library management packages such as LibSys, Virtua, Alice for Windows, KOHA, etc., for automation will also eradicate the fear of errors as these standard packages are installed at a number of large academic and special libraries in India.

Extensive Training

A thorough and extensive training of professional staff of libraries is essential for a good conversion to a good automation project. The training should always be in both oral demonstration and written records wherein the queries raised about the functioning of different automated operations are answered to librarians' satisfaction. A manual or instruction book will always be very helpful for professionals to know about the new system and new working environment. These training tools should always be kept up-to-date. Freshers' coming into the library shall be trained from very beginning in the system. Materials/contents regarding automation projects shall also be sent to the mass media and leading local newspapers for garnering interest among the learned society towards automating libraries. Such trends and tools will not only acquaint the users in learning how to use automated libraries, but will also turn out to be excellent publicity promotions to draw new users towards the libraries.

Nonetheless, some scholars with Rowley (1980) notable among them have listed various steps for planning library automation project. These steps include:

Feasibility Studies

The basic objective of feasibility study is to state, analyze and document the data required to make an informed and intelligent decision regarding the technical feasibility, operational feasibility and economic feasibility.

Hiring a Consultant

The purpose of this very step is to help the librarians in planning for automation project. This would comprise developing an infrastructure for interacting with all involved in planning, defining the problem and objectives to be resolved by automation, project cost preparations, needs and assessment, vendor and system performance evaluation, etc. Hiring a skilful and knowledgeable consultant means the successful automation project.

Data Collection and Needs Assessment

The data will be used for different motives like planning an initial budget estimate, providing information for request for proposal and calculating the storage needs for the new automated system, etc. It may be stated here that thoughtful estimates can be sufficient for the planning process.

Examination of Automation Options

The next step in planning an automation project would be to identify the library operations that are to be automated and their order of automation. Here queries like which functions are repetitive and consume much staff time? Which functions need retrieval of information? What are the services that over burden the staff? etc., take place. Take for example the circulation function in a library in which hundreds of books are transacted on daily basis, so this function should get premier attention while planning for automation project. Simply in the planning stage of an automation project, priorities should be set for automation in a phased manner, analysis of hardware, software and other telecommunication infrastructure required for the purpose and developing a budget for automation project.

Bibliographic Database Development

There are some basic steps involved in establishing a complete bibliographic database of a particular library's holding and to make these databases serviceable. These steps would be:

- Identify, describe and documenting the existing shelf list for standardizing the data they possess.
- Establish the quality ccntrol measures for ensuring the uniformity of data within the prepared shelf list file.
- Record the prepared holdings.
- Validate the existing bibliographic information in the shelf list file.
- Locate and add the compulsory missing bibliographic information, if any.
- Use uniform standard cataloguing practices.
- Prepare specifications for treatment of bibliographic data and item data.
- Prepare and distribute a request for proposal for vendor supplied data conversion project.
- Assess the proposals and chose a vendor.

- Systematize the staff and describe the measures for working with vendor to decide the bibliographic record difference, if any.

System Specification and Requirements

The request for proposal with specifications for an automated system shall be prepared in such a way that it will meet the objectives and requirements of a particular library. A good request for proposal will always impress the vendors to detail the costs in such a manner as to make the comparison of different vendors possible for specific configuration. This request for proposal shall be distributed among the appropriate vendors of library automation industry. It is also advised that the collected data may be broken into functional specifications which will describe the desired capabilities in a system and technical specifications which will deal with the standards to be adhered for ensuring minimum system performance. In addition, preparing criteria by which proposals will be analysed and evaluated is also recommended.

Analyse Proposals and Select the Vendor

This step of planning an automation project would include the following basic tasks:

- Assessing the vendor proposals
- Preparing the queries for vendor supplied contacts
- Call vendor references and interview them
- Chose some top proposals
- Organize some onsite demonstrations by Vendors
- Motivate the selection committee to make the site visit to the system
- Ask the top vendors to discuss about their experiences working with the system to be implemented
- Prepare and raise some queries to vendors during the demonstration
- Analyse the output of vendor presentation

Start the Agreement and Negotiations with the Top Chosen Vendor

Here the issues like library specifications, vendor performance, warranties, vendor bankruptcy, software infringement, annual maintenance charges, request for proposal in contract, setting contract negotiation agenda, bringing negotiations to a successful conclusion and other related issues are discussed. The basic task involved in this step of planning an automation project would be to involve legal counsel and library personnel for assessing the actual contract for its implementation.

Implement the System

Prior to implementation of the selected system, a benchmark test would ideally be advised. Pertinently, the benchmark tests need careful planning and preparation and should be devised with legal counsel. Sometimes, benchmark tests are time consuming and a costly affair and, therefore, they should not be automatically required for every vendor replying to the request for proposal. The typical performance tests to be conducted prior to implementation of a selected system would include system reliability test, functional performance acceptance test and response time test. The system reliability test assures that the system is entirely operational for the time specified in the request for proposal. The functional performance test confirms that the system capability can execute as per the functional requirements drafted in the request for proposal. In case of response time test, it decides whether the system can achieve the intended functions within the required response time under a full transaction load agreed in the request for proposal (Rowley, 1980).

However, some other scholars have suggested following steps in the planning of library automation in Indian libraries:

- Justification, here librarians have to justify the various wonderful benefits and some disadvantages that automation will bring with itself.
- System analysis, as an introduction to automation, in which analysis of needs, the present operations, operating setting, inputs and outputs are done.
- Identification of the library operations to be automated.
- Designing an automated system. It is here system analysts and technical specialists are called for a good design of automated system, though presently many automated and readymade designs are available online.
- Procuring of hardware.
- Procuring the appropriate library software package, since different libraries have different needs.
- Budget, it is most vital part which should be thoroughly discussed before planning the project. Costing of the present system to be compared with costing of the new proposed system taking due account of benefits of the automated systems.
- Pilot study is important before implementation of the automation project. It gives the direction to the project and helps in identifying and eradicating the errors, if any by testing the different operations of the project. In simple words, pilot study is the implementation of the project at a small scale.
- Implementing the project entirely after the successful pilot study.
- Evaluation of the system.

Nevertheless, it has been seen that a fairly good automation project can untimely turn into a disaster of things, if it is not properly planned, properly designed and properly implemented. The poor planning, poor designing and poor implementation will be huge loss of investment, intellectual effort and share wastage of all the important time. It is, therefore, equally advised that the librarians' shall be very careful during the different stages of planning and implementing an effective and successful automation project. Besides, it is also suggested that the professional staff of libraries which are intending for automating their operations and services, shall undergo a detailed and thorough training on all different modules of a standard library package selected for automating library system. Care shall also be taken prior to selecting a library software package by involving top vendors of the library automation industry for evaluating different leading library management systems, before implementing blindly any library automation package. In simple words, it can be stated that library automation is not an overnight preparation, but an exhaustive, intellectual and combining effort of skilful librarian, dedicated project leader, content specialist, experienced technique specialist, capable system analysts and designer, professional programmer and above all a qualitative manager. The qualitative, vibrant and interactive participation of all these persons can ensure effective, efficient and successful automation project in libraries.

HARDWARE AND SOFTWARE REQUIREMENTS FOR AUTOMATION

Hardware of the computer consists of central processing unit and other related outer devices. The central processor executes the main function of computing and comprises the arithmetic control and other memory circuit. The peripheral devices execute the functions like input, output or other auxiliary storage operations. These memory circuits are meant for the storage of data and other programs with which a computer system operates at a given time. It may be defined here that these data and programs are encoded in a computer readable language often called as binary language. These binary forms are represented by a series of bits of verifying breadths. The physical demonstration of these binary bits differs with the type of memory components used in the computer system. The new computer systems are represented by the features like semiconductor memories wherein the individual characters are demonstrated either by presence or absence of electric current in a definite arrangement of circuits. The modern day computer's memory is determined in multiples of 1024 bytes (equivalent to 1 MB, mega bits) or characters. The recent developments in computer technology have made the earlier large sized mainframe computers possible in small sized mini and then microcomputers. In simple words, the full sized computers are better operated by centralized data processing facilities, while the minicomputers are better to be implemented in decentralized departments. In case of libraries, minicomputers are majorly meant for particular functions such as circulation activities (Saffady, 1983). Microcomputers on the other hand are more properly intended for office or desk level.

SYSTEM REQUIREMENTS

Selecting a suitable and appropriate computer system for libraries has always been a challenging task for librarians. A college or university library is primarily required to settle what type of computer is most suitable to their library operations and services, since there is a variety of computers' ranging from mini-frame to mainframe and microcomputers and then personal computers. Notably, these personal computers often taken as PCs are categorized into following four types:

- Personal Computers (PCs),
- Personal Computers- Extended Intermediate Technology (PC-XT),
- Personal Computers – Advanced Technology (PC-AT), and

- Personal Computers –Super Advanced Technology (PC-Super-AT) (Galhotra, 2008).

Of these four types of computers, a college or university libraries, because of their large library system, would require personal computers-advance technology (PC-AT), though PC-XT can also serve the purpose.

HARDWARE REQUIREMENTS

Hardware is often taken as the combination of main constituents of a computer which are tangible and mostly attached externally to the computer system. These constituents include :

1. Input devices,
2. Central Processing Unit,
3. Backup storage also called as auxiliary storage, and
4. Output devices.

All these devices have been discussed one by one in detail hereafter.

1. INPUT DEVICES

These devices actually read the data from a particular form and then convert it into electrical pulses. These electrical pulses are then transmitted into an input location in the Central Processing Unit. The data entered into the main memory is termed as inputting. The input devices actually make possible users to translate their data into binary language and send to computer processer. These devices are possible to be attached/ detached/reattached to the computer as and when required and are hence termed as peripherals. The different kinds of input devices are keyboard, card readers, tape drive, disk drive, optical character recognition, joystick, mouse, light pen, scanner, magnetic scanners, pointing devices, sensor devices (voice), barcodes, and image processing, etc. However, the worth noting input devices comprise the following:

Punched Cards

Punched cards are often taken for both input and external memory or storage medium. They are the most traditional form of inputting and storage mediums used by the libraries. Nevertheless, the emergence of fast and less space consuming input devices of modern days have thrown these punched cards out of the gear and race. Punched cards have been discussed earlier in chapter-1 also.

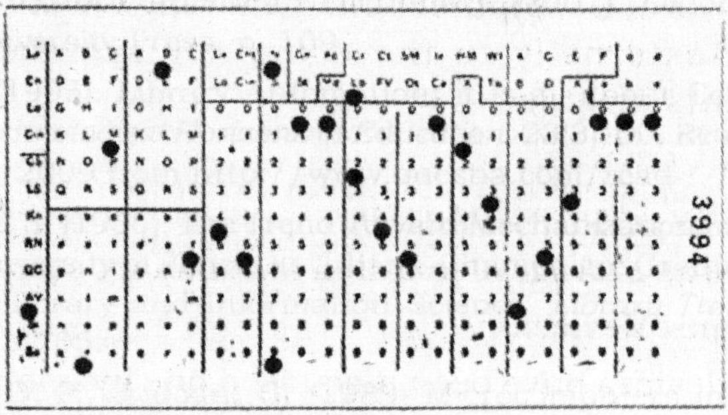

(a)

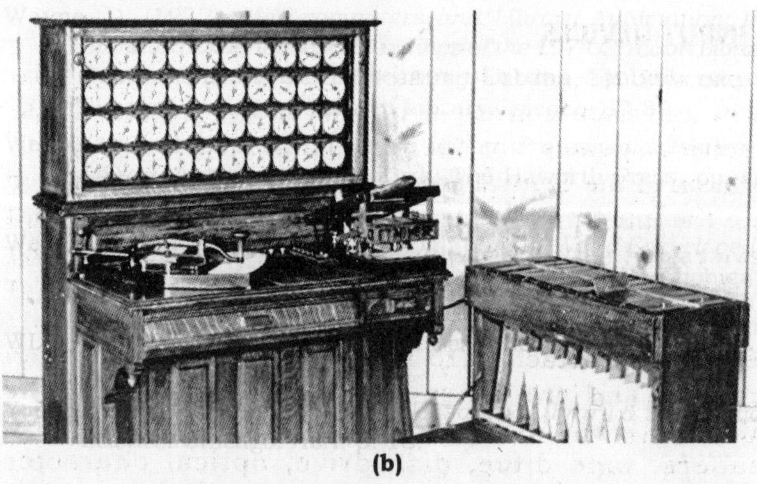

(b)

Fig. 1. (a) Diagrammatic representation of Punched Cards (b) Punched Card Tabulators (*Image Courtesy IBM 100 Icons of Progress*)

Magnetic Disc Drum

It is a generally used internal storage medium. In this case, the drum is like a cylinder that is mounted on a shaft spinned by a motor at a very fast speed. These disc drums make possible the direct access to the required data. The space of the drum is layered with metallic oxide enabling the face of drum to be magnetized in tiny distinct areas of cells. The beauty of disc drum is that the data speed in it is very fast.

Fig. 2. Diagrammatic representation of Magnetic Disc Drums (*Image Courtesy The Free Dictionary by Farlex*)

Magnetic Tapes

It is an input storage medium made of half an inch plastic having magnetic oxide covering surface on one side. The data is entered and retrieved with the support of read/ write heads. Magnetic tapes resembles to the tape of a usual tape recorder. It may be stated here that magnetic tapes possess relatively vast storing capacity. It can hold 2500 characters on each centimetre of the tape. It also facilitates the users to delete or erase the wrong or old data with the new data. However, dust particles and humidity are its enemies and lessens its life.

Fig. 3. Diagrammatic representation of Magnetic Tape

Optical Disks

They are new option to magnetic storage. In it, digital data is burn into surface of a plastic disk covered with a low wetting point metal by a laser beam. The appearance or nonappearance of a hole communicates to one bit and can be read by another laser. Like magnetic tapes, optical disks have huge storage capacity at low cost and in a form permitting quick access.

WORM

Write once Read Many times disks are perfect for archival purpose as they allow to storage huge amount of data on one disk. However, the main issue with WORM technology is that it lacks of any industry standards.

CD-ROM

Compact Disk Read Only Memory until recently was major means of distributing databases and documentation. However, with the newer means of data storage devices, their use has diminished to a considerable extent.

Floppy Disks

Floppy disk is a smooth coated with magnetic surface which has tracks on it. In floppy disks, data can be created or read in it as a sequence of magnetic pulses. However, floppy disks are now rarely used by libraries and their users, since other forceful means of information storage devices with huge quantity of storage capacity have emerged in the market.

Microforms

Libraries are now substituting the traditional books and newspapers by means of microforms and microfiches. They are comparatively less in cost than the paper and are easy to distribute. Nevertheless, Indian libraries are still giving emphasis to physical collection, though newer technology is easily available. It apparently seems that Indian libraries will take much time for shifting from accessing of physical collection to electronic collection, though some university libraries and research libraries have been developing electronic collection from some years now.

Fig. 4. Diagrammatic representation of Microfilm (*Image Courtesy NIFHS.org*)

Fig. 5. Diagrammatic representation of Microfilm Reader

Fig. 6. Diagrammatic representation of Microfiches

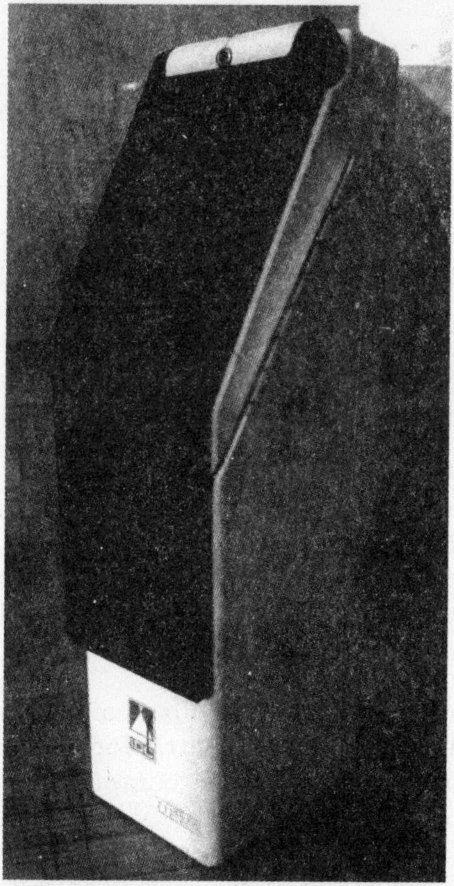

Fig. 7. Diagrammatic representation of Microfiche Reader

Optical Storage Discs

These input devices make use of laser beams to both record as well as read backup data stored on a photo sensitive medium of a disc. It is one of the latest developments in storage devices. Optical storage discs comprise three kinds of functional varieties. These include

Read Only Optical Discs

This is a publishing and distribution media as it enables a user to only read the data by inserting the disc in a player. The facility of recording the data is restricted in these discs. One of the common examples of read only optical discs is CD-ROM which stores the data on the disc by a high powered laser. It is able to read by a CD-ROM reader that is connected to a benchmark micro-computer.

Write Once Optical Discs

These types of optical discs can be used for low volume data distribution. This data is possible to be recorded into the disc over a period of time till the disc is full. The main shortcoming of this type of disc is that any sector of the disc is possible to be written once only and the data cannot be erased or overwritten.

Erasable Rewritable Optical Discs

In this type of disc, the recording process is possible to be reversed. The main advantage of erasable rewritable optical discs is that the data is possible to be deleted with new data recorded on the same sectors of the disc.

2. CENTRAL PROCESSING UNIT

This is often called as physical part of the computer that controls all the computer functions. This is rightly regarded as the brain of the computer. It consists of following three different constituents including the control unit, the arithmetic logic unit and the main memory. All these three are made of microelectronic devices which are nearly based on silicon semiconductor technology.

Control Unit

This part of the computer digs out program commands in the desired sequence from their locations in the main memory. It then decides and directs the commands to access the needed word or information and then to the arithmetic unit to activate the required instructions circuitry.

Arithmetic Unit

The arithmetic part of the computer includes a set of registers or accumulators which mainly perform the desired calculations in a speed never imagined before. This register is normally attached with circuitry which conducts the hundreds of fundamental operations available to the computer.

Main Memory

Main memory is considered as the largest constituent of a central processing unit. It is further divided into individual words with each of them able to be accessed individually by its address. It may be stated here that all modern computers are based on semiconductor technology which possesses the power to place thousands of electronic components inside a restricted area of silicon. The main memory also called as primary storage constitute the major part of central processing unit and controls the program commands and data required as per the programs operate.

3. BACKUP STORAGE/AUXILIARY STORAGE

Primarily there are two kinds of storages, the internal storage that lies inside the CPU and the backup storage that are connected externally like disks or tapes. Both these kinds are discussed hereunder.

Internal Storage

This storage is also called as core storage or main storage and is used to clutch those commands and data that is needed at any point of time while a program is operated. For internal storage, silicon semi conductor chips are now invariably used. It may be mentioned here that these chips are either Random Access Memory (RAM) or Read Only Memory (ROM) chips. The measuring unit for internal storage is bits or bytes.

Backup Storage

Also called as external storage, it is used to control the programs and data which are read into internal storage as and when required. The most common examples in this regard are that of magnetic storage media, tapes or disks. Magnetic tapes are mostly used for storing huge amount of data for which swift access is not essential particularly for archival data backups, etc. Though these tapes are less costly for storing data, but the access to this data is usually low. On contrary, magnetic disks are popularly used backing storage for controlling data/ information required rapidly such as data for operating a program. In case of a disk drive in large computers, data/ information is recorded on the plane surfaces of stack of rounded disks spinning on a common spindle with one read/write head for each disk. However, smaller computers use Winchester disk which are restricted in storage capability.

4. OUTPUT DEVICES

The output unit of computer transmits information from CPU and converts the electrical pulses to output form. Some of the well known output devices include printer, visual display unit, etc. It is mostly based on cathode ray tube, but has clearly improved the quality with reduced price.

Printer

These are most popular output devices found in almost all libraries. These are main output devices used to make a permanent document in man readable form in hard copies. By hard copy, the author means to say the printed copy of the processed data usually in a computer. There are several kinds of printers such as line printers, page printers, etc. However, one classification categorizes printers broadly into impact printers and non impact printers. The different types of printers have been discussed as under.

Character Printer

These printers print just single character at a time like typewriter does. The other kinds of character printers are letter quality printers, dot matrix printers and inkjet printers which are accordingly described as under:

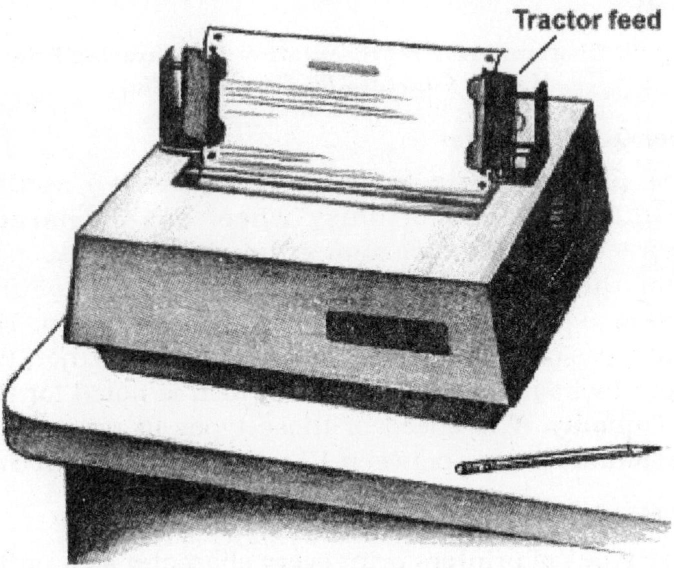

Fig. 8. Diagrammatic representation of Old Character Printer (*Image Courtesy PC Encyclopedia*)

Fig. 9. Diagrammatic representation of Character Printer (*Image Courtesy PC Encyclopedia*)

Letter Quality Printer

These printers use a print wheel also known as Daisy Wheel. Each petal of daisy wheel has a character imprinted on it. A motor rotates the wheel at a fast speed. When the required character rotates the accurate position, a print hammer hit it to create the output. Thus these types of printers are impact printers. Further, their output looks like a typed output which is noted for their print quality. The speed of these types of printers has been found ranging between 10 to 50 characters/second.

Dot Matrix Printer

These types of printers print every character as a pattern of dots. The print head in dot matrix printer contain a matrix of little needles containing seven rows with nine needles in each. These hammer out the character in the shape of pattern of little dots. The shape of these little dots is obtained from the information controlled electronically in the system. The print quality of this type of printer is questionable as that of daisy wheel, but dot matrix printers are usually faster than letter quality printers and are less expensive. Nevertheless in a set up like libraries, quality is difficult to comprise with and hence librarians should think twice before procuring dot matrix printers (Galhotra, 2008).

Fig. 10. Diagrammatic representation of Letter Quality Printer (*Image Courtesy Computer History Museum*)

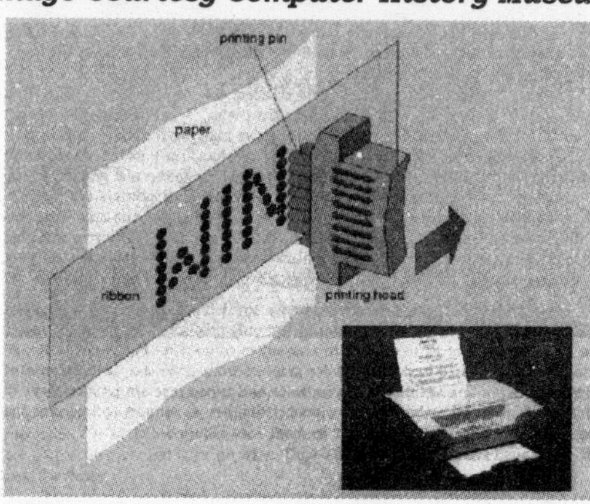

Fig. 11. Diagrammatic representation of Dot Matrix Printer (*Diagram Courtesy Google Images*)

Inkjet Printers

These are non-impact printers made of new technology. An inkjet printer consists of a print head comprising a number of little holes or nozzles. Ink wells control ink near these nozzles. Individual wells can be heated quickly by an integrated circuit resistor. On resistors heating, the ink near it is expelled via the nozzle and sprays dots on paper positioned near the head. A high resolution inkjet printer has usually 50 nozzles with 7mm height and is able to print with a resolution of 300 dots/inch. Colour inkjet printers make use of three different inkjets, one for each of the main colours like red, green and blue. On combination of fitting colours, all colours are created (Rajaraman and Adabala, 2015). Inkjet printers alongwith other non impact printers have restriction in creating multiple copies of a document/book in a single printing. It may be mentioned here that impact character printers have this kind of facility. The diagrammatic representation of inkjet printer is shown below.

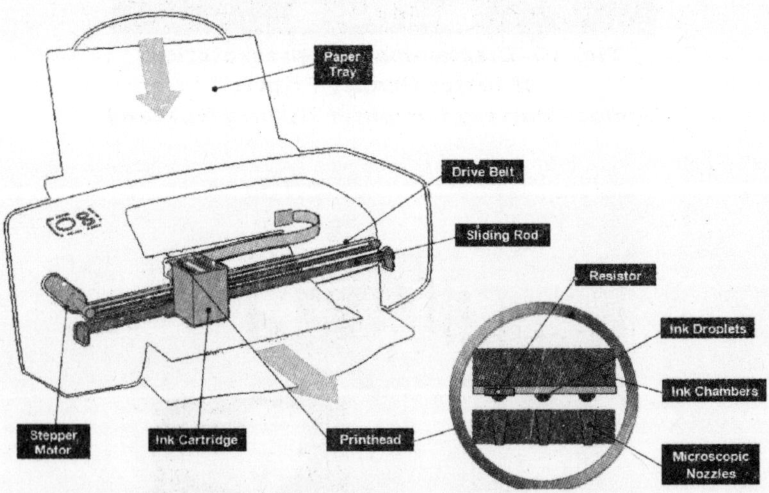

Fig. 12. Diagrammatic representation of Inkjet Printer (*Diagram Courtesy Google Images*)

Line Printers

These are impact printers and are used with most medium and large computer systems for creating huge quantity paper output. They are swift printers with speed ranging between 300-2500 lines/minute. The output effectiveness of these printers is possible to be enhanced by using multi-user papers when more than single copy of the output is required. Some of the popular line printers are drum printer and chain printer which are further explained below.

Fig. 13. Diagrammatic representation of Line Printer (*Image Courtesy IPSJ Computer Museum 2015*)

Drum Printer

It consists of a solid cylindrical drum with raised characters in bands on its face. There are as many bands as there are printing positions. Thus each band consist all the potential characters. It may be explained here that the drum spins at a very quick speed. Further for each potential print position, that is to say opposite to each drum, there is a print hammer positioned at the back of the paper. These hammers hit the paper along with the inked ribbon against the appropriate character on the drum as it goes by it. One revolution of the drum is needed to print each line. This indicates that all the characters on the line are not printed simultaneously; nevertheless, the time needed to produce the whole line is as quick as to call them line printers. It may be mentioned here that the distinctive speed of drum printers range between 300 to 2000 lines/minute.

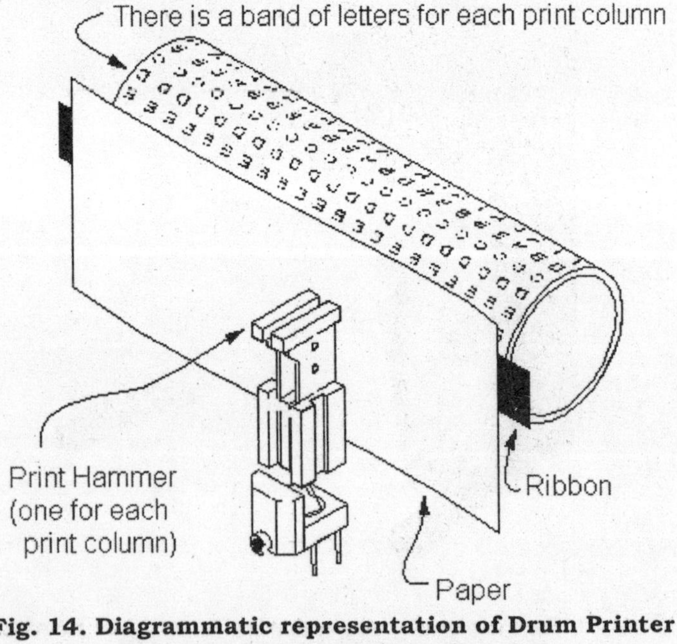

Fig. 14. Diagrammatic representation of Drum Printer (*Image Courtesy PC Encyclopedia*)

Chain Printer

They use a quickly moving chain and hence known as chain printers. Here each connection of the chain is a characters font. However, some models use metal band containing elevated print characters on it. It is worth noting here that for each possible print position, there is a point hammer located at the back of the paper. As the print chain or band spins, the appropriately timed print hammers hit the paper alongwith the inked ribbon against the appropriate character on the chain or band as it goes by. For improving the quickness of chain printers, the character set is repeated many times on the chain. The speed of the chain printers usually range between 400 to 2500 characters/minute.

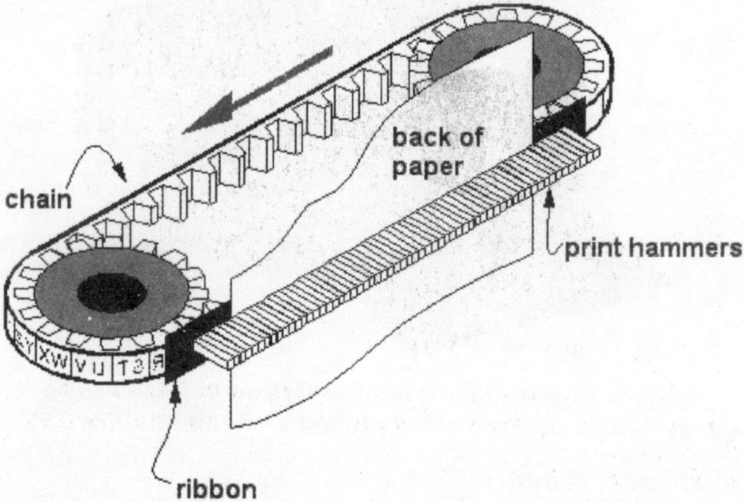

Fig. 15. Diagrammatic representation of Chain Printer (*Image Courtesy PC Encyclopedia*)

Page Printers

These are very high speed non impact printers with ability to create the documents at a speed of above 20,000 lines/ minute. Electronics, xerography lasers and other technologies have made these high volume systems possible. It is pointed out here that page printers are in a position to create pages of output at a rate equal to a paper copier. Moreover, each page created on these types of printers is an original, since it does not contain carbon copies. However, page printers have been found relatively costlier and are suggested only when there is the requirement of printing thousands of pages monthly. Below is the diagrammatic representation of page printer.

Fig. 16. Diagrammatic representation of Page Printer
(*Image Courtesy Marruttusa Inkjet Excellence since 1995*)

Non Impact Printers

These printers constitute electrostatic printers, xerographic printers, laser printers and inkjet printers. The electrostatic printers use a dot matrix of print via which an electronic current is sent. Inkjet printers create hard copy by controlling ink drops with an electronic pulse or by spraying ink from nozzles contained in the print head. On the other hand, Laser printer applies a laser beam to mark out characters or images into light sensitive drum which attracts the toner that sticks to the paper in the form outlined by the laser (Galhotra, 2008).

Plotters

This is another valuable output device. It facilitates drawing of lines, curves, graphs, charts, engineering drawings, maps, pictures and other complex shapes there are two types of plotters, the drum plotter and the flatbed plotter. In case of drum plotter, the paper is mounted on a spinning drum. A pen capable of moving linearly to the route of a drum spinning is mounted on a carriage. The drum is possible to spin clockwise or anticlockwise under the command of plotting instructions sent by the system. Besides moving left to right and right to left, the pen also moves up and down. These movements of pen are administered by the graph of plotting program. The program, therefore, draws a number of drawings and also

Fig. 17. Diagrammatic representation of Plotter
(*Image Courtesy : Impact Computer Trading LLC*)

interprets them by using the pen to draw characters. On the other hand, a flatbed plotter has an unmoving flat plotting surface on which paper is fixed. The pen is mounted on carriage which can move in x or y direction. Besides, the pen can also move up and down. A graph plotting program is used to move the pen to trace the required drawing (Rajaraman and Ababala, 2015).

Thus there are many kinds of printers available in the market. It is, however, suggested that librarians shall get in thoughtful consultation with technique specialists for selecting the printers, output and input devices that mostly suit their library requirements in a better and effective way.

In a set up like libraries, the most input operations depend on key board oriented devices at which data/ information is entered character by character. The oldest of the keyboard oriented input devices is keypunch which converts the independently entered characters to a particularly designed fashion of holes, punched in successive columns of a specially designed card. However, the newer technologies like optical character recognition scan the documents with the facility to convert their contents into machine readable form automatically. Similarly, bar coded label is used in some library circulation systems. Further, the optical character recognition (OCR) which is used to recognize the individual character content of input documents, finds more utility if documents are entered in a font that is particularly designed for identification by computers. A different form of optical character recognition technology i.e. image digitization is used for the conversion of graphic documents to computer readable form (Saffady, 1983). Pertinently, many Indian libraries through the financial assistance of ministry of information communication and technology presently digitize the rare and thesis collection by using the image digitizing form of optical character recognition technology.

The output devices convert computer processed data into man readable form for its ultimate use. In libraries, the output information may be printed, recorded on microfilm or at times displayed on the monitor. There are some devices which are in a position to print accented characters, non Roman alphabets and other symbols encountered in libraries bibliographic data.

In case of hardware requirements for automation, a library may have its own computer for processing its work on its own system housed usually in a separate room in the library. This approach is, however, mainly meant for large libraries which have huge collection and bears to afford its own computers. Most of the Indian libraries are able to use the computers only, if they share the use of machines with other libraries. However, with the falling price of hardware and software requirements, more Indian libraries are tempted towards the use of computerized library system. Nevertheless, it is seen that many Indian librarians' posses less knowledge and less experience and thus fail to manage a highly technical support system for effective automation.

As soon as library starts for automating, the involvement with hardware and software may take on several different forms. The principal arrangement in this direction varies from one application to another. In some applications, there is less choice in hardware and software arrangement, while in others; a particular library with reasonably wide-ranging automation will perhaps depend on more than one arrangement. But one vital element in the planning and selection process should be library's consciousness of merits and demerits of the available types of arrangements.

Reynolds has identified most common types of hardware and software arrangements for automated library systems. In any online automated library system, the library would be required to have some type of in-house infrastructure, such as terminals, but the choices given by Reynolds more particularly concern the setting of actual processing unit itself.

Table 1. Reynolds Hardware and Software Arrangement in Library Automation

	Main Computer Location		
Application Software Source	Central Site of Library Automation Vendor	Computer Centre of Library's Parent Institution	In the Library
System Developed Remotely	Remote access; eg. Bibliographic utilities, information retrieval services, serials subscription agents, acquisition book jobbers	Purchase of software from vendor or another library to run on large mainframe or minicomputer	Turnkey system: hardware and software purchased from one source
			Purchase of hardware and software from different sources
Software developed through local computer centre		Local system: software developed by local computer centre and run on its equipment	
Software developed by library			Strictly in-house system; most commonly found with micro computer applications

It is seen that the horizontal rows in the above table differentiate amid different approaches to the development of application software. In some instances, libraries may have hardware and software arrangements somewhat dissimilar from those appeared above in the table. The above constituted matrix as per Reynolds results in many possible hardware software combinations, though some are conflicting by definition, while some are very unlikely. Nevertheless, many are fairly common in library automation.

The hardware and computing environment required for library automation can differ from easy to very complex and economical to very expensive, depending largely on the operations to be performed and the number of users to be served, compatibility to standards and the linking to external sources or bibliographic databases. Some of the requirements for automation project as per Haravu are discussed below:

SINGLE-USER SYSTEMS

In single user system environment, the user has a display terminal linked to a computer and a disk drive that contains the application programs and databases. There is also a possibility of a local printer and CD drive linked to the computer. In this specific configuration, the user adds records to the database, searches the catalogue, displays retrieved information and then creates printed output. Such a configuration can be used as a foundation for more complex ones or stand alone systems.

MULTI-USER SYSTEMS

In this kind of configuration, there is possibility of many users accessing the computer system that contains automation applications and other related data files. A level of complexity is added in multi-user systems as the system should handle simultaneous access to database with special mention that no two users should enter the same record at a time. This kind of configuration also requires a particular hardware often known as terminal server to handle the transmission and receipt of data amid the central processing unit and the user terminals. The multi-user system configuration is largely designed for centralized mainframe and minicomputer architecture.

LOCAL AREA NETWORKS (LANs)

In library automation project, another configuration of hardware requirements could be local area network which is a system of interacting within a campus, a building or closely situated buildings. The growth of standard networking protocols and media has produced global explosion of LANs throughout many organizations including libraries. In this system, each node has its personal CPU, though it also has the ability to access data and devices anywhere on the LAN. This provision permits several users to share expensive devices. Besides, users are also able to link with one another user through e-mail or chat sessions in this system of configuration. Further, LANs are also able to transmit data at very faster rates than normal telephone cables. However, the distances possible to be covered through LANs are limited. There is also limit on the number of nodes or computer terminals attached to a single LAN.

The LAN system also appends to the network, a dominant workstation known as server that stores data and transports data and programs to user workstations. These LANs are constituted of coaxial cables, or fibre optic cables or twisted pair cables. The other hardware requirements on LAN could be specific function printers and CD-ROM towers which permit users to share printers on the network. LANs are based on file sharing architectures in which the server downloads files from the shared location to the desktop environment. Further, the application software lives on the server which is brought into action by the users at several different terminals. The programs are afterwards performed on the user nodes. A LAN also requires a terminal server to handle link among user terminals and network server. It may be mentioned here that personal computers dependent LANs need a network operating system or software which improves a main operating system by adding networking features. The shortcomings of LAN mentioned earlier have led to the development of client server architecture which is the requirement of most modern library management packages for automation.

CLIENT SERVER ARCHITECTURE

This term was for the first time used in 1980s with special mention of personal computers on the network. However, it gained the momentum during the decade of late 80s. The client server architecture is multitalented message based and modular infrastructure that is planned to enhance usability, adaptability, interoperability and scalability than centralized, mainframe, time sharing computing.

SOFTWARE REQUIREMENTS FOR LIBRARY AUTOMATION

Software is the soft version of written programs, characteristics, purchase and management of programs and programming effort associated with the library automation. According to Haravu, Library automation systems are application softwares that primarily need other software for the desired work to be accomplished. However, some library automation software functions only under a special operating system. While there are some vendors which provide the same software under more than one operating system. It is also seen that most of the high end software structure are sometimes attached to a particular server like Oracle or MS-SQL Server. In such a case, the library application software will need a license to implement and run Database Management System on its server. Also the software that functions under a special operating system mostly needs small software like Dynamic Link Libraries or ActiveX components (Haravu, 2004). These may be the softwares that often require many applications under the operating systems or are particularly produced for library automation software. Furthermore, the web based library automation software may also need a special web server for the appropriate working of several modules. Some softwares may also ask for run time modules of special software like Java to be installed for several modules to work appropriately. It may be pointed out here that the library automation software packages are broadly described in the chapter 3 of this book.

Though some university libraries and special libraries particularly those catering the needs of Research and Development organizations have been doing fairly good job in automating their library system on American and British lines, nevertheless, it is a general realization that the status of automation in majority of Indian libraries is not encouraging. In this direction, the onus comes on various professional associations and networks including Information and Library Network (IFLIBNET), Indian Library Association which is more powerful in its abbreviated form (ILA), Indian Association of Special Libraries and Information Centres (IASLIC), Developing Libraries Network (DELNET), Indian Association of Teachers in Library and Information Science (IATLIS), Raja Rom Mohan Roy Library Foundation (RRLF), National Library, Kolkata and other reputed Indian library science schools for fully supporting both financially, technically and professionally the cause of standardization and automation of Indian libraries on modern lines.

REFERENCES

Computer History Museum (2015). *Artefact Details: Letter Quality Printers*. Retrieved Dec 24, 2015 from http://www.computerhistory.org/collections/catalog/102682758

Galhotra, M.K. (2008). *Information Technology in Library and Information Services*. New Delhi: ESS ESS, pp. 67-81

Haravu, L. J. (2004). *Library Automation Design, Principles and Practice*. New Delhi: Allied, pp. 34-37, 69-150.

IBM 100 Icons of Progress (2015). *The Punched Card Tabulator.* Retrieved Dec 20, 2015 from http://www-03.ibm.com/ibm/history/ibm100/us/en/icons/tabulator/ing&imgrc=3D7MsGKQlrTlqM%3A

Impact Computer Trading (2015). *Plotters.* Retrieved Dec. 17, 2015 from http://www.impactauh.ae/plotters/

Inkjet Printer (2015) Retrieved Dec 20, 2015 from https://www.google. co.in/search?q=inkjet+printer&espv= 2&biw=1066&bih= 477&site=webhp&source=lnms &tbm=isch&sa=X&ved= 0ahUKEwj lgqvdu4DLAhXIBI4KHZ3VBOgQ_AUIBigB#tbm= isch&q=inkjet+printer+work

IPSJ Computer Museum (2015). *Historical Computers in Japan* Printers Retrieved Dec. 17, 2015 from http://museum.ipsj.or.jp/en/computer/device/printer/0007.html

Marruttusa, inkjet excellence (1995) *Professional Inkjet Solutions.* Retrieved Dec 24 , 2015 from http://www.marruttusa.com/printer/epson-r1900.php

Moore, E. (1967) System Analysis: An Overview. *Special Libraries.* 58, 87-90.

NIFHS (2015). *North of Ireland Family History Society: Microfiches and Microfilms.* Retrieved Dec 23, 2015 from http://www.nifhs.org/resources/microfiches-microfilms/

Oyemankinde, A. (July, 1979). Automation at Ibadan University Library. *Program,* 3(3), 143-146.

PC Encyclopedia (2015). Home/how to/Encyclopedia. Retrieved Dec. 17, 2015 from http://www.pcmag.com/encyclopedia/term/42019/drum-printer

Rajaraman, V., & Adabala, N. (2015). *Fundamentals of Computers (6th ed.).* New Delhi: PHI Learning, p. 48.

Rajgopalan, G. (1981). Computerized Book Acquisition. *Journal of Library and Information Science,* 6(2), 84-91.

Reynolds, D. (1985). *Library Automation Issues and Applications.* New York: R. R. Bowker, pp. 29-408.

Rowley, J.E. (1980). Planning and Designing of Computerized Library. *In Computers for Libraries* (2nd ed.). London: The Library Association.

Saffady, W. (1983). Introduction to Automation for Librarians. Chicago: American Library Association, pp. 3-35.

Swihart, S., & Hefley, B. F. (1973). *Computer Systems in the Library:*

a Handbook for Managers & Designers. California: Melville, PP. 246-270.

The Free dictionary by Farlex (2015) *Magnetic Drum*. Retrieved Dec 20, 2015 from http://encyclopedia2.thefreedictionary.com/magnetic+drum

Dot Matrix Printer (2015). Retrieved Dec 20, 2015 from https://www.google.co.in/search?q=dot+matrix+printer&espv=2&biw=1066&bih= 477&source=l nms&tbm=isch&sa=X&ved=0ahUKEwiZ24zk34 DLAhUEc44KHTMsDgkQ_AUIBigB&dpr=1.5#tbm=isch&q=dot+matrix+printer+ working&imgrc=XFsS5ie2SOAg6M%3A

3

Popular Library Management Systems in India

Many library software packages were developed in India, however, because of their incompatibility with international standards, most of these packages could not survived in present day automated environment. Consequently, a number of large Indian academic and special libraries switched over to international software packages to overcome these drawbacks of indigenous packages. This chapter throws light on different software packages popularly used by Indian university libraries for automating their operations and services.

BACKGROUND

Software is a set of programs written or developed to enable the computer to do some desired operations. Application software is a software, developed or written, to enable the computer, to carry out some specific functions, required by a particular group of users. Library automation software packages are application softwares that contains modules for all the specific activities that may concern a particular user group like a software containing modules for acquisition work, cataloguing, circulation, serials control and documentation, etc. (Sharma, 1993). Though research centres and special libraries of the nation were primer in the development of library software packages, but most of their packages could not satisfy either library or user needs effectively, and hence did not last long. Nonetheless with the fast development in software industry both at national and international level, a number of commercial library software management packages with integrated modules and other standard features became available through different software vendors. However, in this work, an effort has been made to discuss the following most popularly used library software packages by Indian libraries.

- SOUL (Software for University Libraries)
- Granthalaya Software
- LibSys Software
- Alice for Windows Software
- Suchika Software
- Maitreyi Software
- Sanjay Software
- Virtua Software
- LIBRIS Software
- TULIPS Software
- Librarian Software
- WINISIS Software
- MINISIS Software, etc.

A detailed summary of these library software packages has been given hereunder with respect to their modules, standards, features and other operationlization aspects; besides their popularity viz number of installations/ libraries using the software across the country.

SOUL SOFTWARE

The acronym SOUL stands for Software for University Libraries and is developed by an inter university centre namely Information and Library Network (INFLIBNET) with its head office in Ghandinagar, Ahmedabad. It is integrated library management software meant to automate the college and university libraries of India. SOUL is basically a Windows version of integrated library management system (ILMS) which was specially designed by INFLIBNET in collaboration with Defence Science Information and Documentation Centre (DESIDOC) to automate university libraries in India. The software is used to automate academic as well as other types of libraries. The centre (INFLIBNET) responsible for design and development of this software provides downloading and mailing list facility to address the problems associated with its installation and operation. The first version of SOUL i.e. SOUL 1.0 appeared during CALIBER conference in the year 2000. While as the latest version, popularly known as SOUL 2.0 emerged in 2009 and is compliant to international standards like MARC 21 for bibliographic format, UNICODE for multi-lingual support, NCIP 2.0 for RFID applications and SIP 2.0 based protocols for electronic surveillance and control (SOUL 2.0, 2014). The availability of new versions of SOUL with robust features and compliance to international standards as that of earlier version, whose compatibility to UNICODE and NCIP in particular was limited, has made it popular among Indian libraries.

Modules

SOUL is known for its following user friendly modules across the country:

- Acquisition
- Catalogue
- Circulation
- Online Public Access Catalogue (OPAC)
- Serials control and
- Administration.

Standards

SOUL is user friendly software, designed on Client-Server architecture. The software is compliant to international standards like: AACR 2; CCF; MARC21; UNICODE support for bi-directional languages; MARCXML; NCIP for RFID applications as stated earlier and ISO 2709 standards for bibliographic formats, networking and circulation protocols.

Platform

SOUL is Client server architecture based. It operates on Windows 98/2000/XP/NT/Windows Vista platforms. The server platform of SOUL runs on Windows 2003 and Windows 2008. This software supports multi platforms for bibliographic databases such as MY SQL, MS-SQL or any other popular Relational Database Management System (RDBMS).

Popularity/Users/Installations

SOUL is most popular library software with more than 2834 libraries in India its clientele till March 2014. Being cost effective and developed primarily to automate the college and university libraries, this software is popularly used across the country by college, university, public and other kinds of libraries for automating their housekeeping operations to provide better and efficient services to their users (INFLIBNET, 2014).

GRANTHALAYA SOFTWARE

It is a complete library automation package, designed and developed in FoxPro language by Indian National Scientific Documentation Centre (INSDOC) New Delhi in 2003. INSDOC is marketing and promoting this package for library automation in Indian libraries and research centres. The package developed further with the emergence of new versions such as e-Granthalaya 2.0 and e-Granthalaya 3.0 (eG3) in 2005 and 2007 respectively. These versions are integrated library management softwares developed by National Informatics Centre, India. This version provides in-built web OPAC interface to publish the library catalogue over Internet. Subduing the shortfalls of earlier version, e-Granthalaya provides UNICODE standard for supporting multiple languages. However, the latest version of e-Granthalaya i.e. Ver.4.0 released sometime in 2015 is a 'Cloud Ready Application' that provides a web-based data entry solution in enterprise mode with a centralized database for cluster of libraries. This latest version uses *PostgreSQL* - an Open Source DBMS as well as Free Edition of MS SQL Server (any version) as back-end database solutions. While as it is available on ASP.NET 4.0/AJAX/JQUERY/JSON/SilverLight platform. In India, e-Granthalaya 4.0 version is made available in NIC National Cloud for Government libraries on request basis where free hosting is provided (e-Granthalaya, 2015). The availability of this package in many latest and modern versions with the facility of integrated library management system and good vendor support services has made many newly established libraries and those libraries which are yet far from automating their operations, to think about this package for switching over to automated library systems.

Modules

Granthalaya contains seven modules. Since the package has different modules, the library can implement either complete package or acquire stand-alone module depending upon the needs of a particular library. The modules of this package are:

- Data administration
- Query circulation
- Acquisition
- Serials control

- Technical processing and
- Library administration

Standards

Granthalaya package is compatible with CCF. It facilitates import and export of data from ISO 2709 for bibliographic formats, besides ASCII format is also possible. The standards viz version wise are also discussed elsewhere in the package.

Platform

Granthalaya package operates both on MS-DOS platform and UNIX platform. The first and second version i.e. 1.0 and 2.0 designed in 2003 and 2005 respectively operates on Visual Basic 6/ASP/HTML platform with MS SQL Server 7 as DBMS in version 1.0 and MS SQL Server 2000 as DBMS in case of version 2.0. The version 3.0, however, operates on VB.NET/ASP.NET 2.0 as platform with MS SQL Server 2005 as DBMS. The latest version namely e-Granthalaya 4.0 is available on ASP.NET4.0/ AJAX/JQUERY/JSON /SilverLight platform with *PostGreSQL*-an Open Source DBMS/Free Edition of SQL Server (any version) as already mentioned in the introduction part. It also supports Z39.50 for communication protocol and AACR 2 to generate bibliography, while it imports records from MARC21/ EXCEL and exports them in CSV/Text File/MARC 21/ MARCXML/ISO: 2709/MS ACCESS/EXCEL formats.

Popularity/Users/Installations

Previously the use of this package was limited to a few libraries in India. Some of the major libraries using Granthalaya software package during that period of time were National Science Library, INSODC (modern NISCAIR), New Delhi and Nuclear Science Centre Library, New Delhi (Saxena & Srivastava, 1998). Since the package has been developed by INSDOC itself, therefore, it retained the package till date for automating its library. However, with the development of new and latest versions like e-Granthalaya 3.0 and e-Granthalaya 4.0, its use has now grown to hundreds of libraries. Being indigenous in nature of its development, it is mainly used by Indian libraries. Notably, the number of users/libraries/installation of this package is higher (roughly about 3200) than other mentioned packages due to its cost effectiveness as compared to LibSys and other foreign packages discussed here (e-Granthalaya, 2015). But, there may be only few large reputed libraries in India which are on its client list. Nevertheless, with the availability of newer versions capable to support international standards, the installation of new eGranthalaya version has taken place in as many as 103 libraries across different States of the India till the fall of 2014.

LIBSYS SOFTWARE

LibSys is an integrated library automation software package developed by Info Consultants Software Company, New Delhi in 1984. The continuous growth and global recognition of LibSys popularized it as a standard package for Indian academic and special libraries. While as open system architecture and continuous transition from host multiuser to client-server and finally web based solution makes LibSys an advanced multi dimensional library system. The features like powerful and user oriented web OPAC along with the Windows based OPAC makes it an outstanding option for library environment not only at national, but at international level. With the compatibility of UNICODE feature i.e. multi-lingual nature, the software handles both Indian as well as international scripts available in bi-directional languages. This package with continuous growth and development has generated LibSys suite comprising different LibSys products like LSEase; LibSys4; LSAcademia; LibSys7; LSPremia; LibSysX,

LSNet; LSmart solutions for RFID applications and LSDigital for digital libraries, LSD&A, etc. All these products are enhanced versions of parent LibSys software with more robust features and compatibility to international standards.

Modules

As integrated library management software, LibSys package supports the following modules:

- Acquisition
- Cataloguing
- Circulation
- Serials control
- Article indexing and
- Online Public Access Catalogue (OPAC)

Standards

LibSys is built around its own centralized bibliographic database on MARC format and therefore supports various types of materials in print as well as non-print form. The software is compatible to international standards such as CCF, USMARC, OCLC, MARC and non MARC formats. Being Indian in origin, LibSys is also compatible with CCC which was devised in 1934 by Shiyali Ramamitra Ranganathan who is more popularly known in short as S.R. Ranganthan and is unanimously considered as father of library science in India.

Platform

LibSys is open system architecture to Client Server. It operates on MS DOS 6.0 and above such as Windows NT, UNIX, Linux and NOVELL platforms. However, it can be made available on any preferred RDBMS such as Oracle or SQL Server. While as LibSys operates on NT/ Unixware/Novell, UNIX, LINUX Sun Sparc (SOLARIS) server platforms.

Popularity (International Users/Installations)

After getting global acknowledgement, LibSys as an integrated library management system is being used in some foreign countries like: National de Universidad, Cost Rica (USA); University of Moratuwa, Sri Lanka; University of Jaffna, Sri Lanka; University of Kelaniya, Kelaniya Sri Lanka; Open University of Sri Lanka, Nawala and Skyline University Sharjah, etc.

National Users/Installations

In India, LibSys is second most popularly used library software package with more than 1000 reputed large libraries presently its clients for automating their library system to provide effective services in an automated environment. Some of the major Indian libraries that use LibSys for automating their housekeeping operations are: IGNOU, New Delhi; AMU, Aligarh; Madras University, Chennai; Allahabad University, Allahabad and Rajasthan University Jaipur, etc. (LibSys Corporation, 2012). LibSys in comparison to other indigenous packages is popularly used by university and college libraries in India.

ALICE FOR WINDOWS SOFTWARE

Alice for Windows is an international integrated library automation package developed in 1983 by Softlink International Company based in Australia. It is marketed through various Office heads based in a number of countries viz. USA, Britain, New Zealand, Australia, Iceland, Singapore, Malaysia, India and Sri Lanka with its offices spread over 100 nations across the globe. However, Softlink Asia promotes this software in India. The software effectively and efficiently manages and controls library operations performing all functions that a modern library system requires. The vast experience of Alice has proven it reliable library package and achieved the status of leading library automation software of the world.

Modules

Alice for Windows is globally known for the robustness of its modules. The software contain following modules:

- Acquisition
- Circulation
- Management
- Periodicals
- Journal indexing
- Multimedia
- Multilingual
- Subject authority
- Web enquiry
- Book hire, and Patron self check

Besides the main modules, union catalogue; inter library loan; rapid retro; SDI; Z39.50 server and library services are some sub modules of Alice for Windows.

Standards

Alice for Windows supports USMARC format; E-resource cataloguing; web-OPAC; MARC import/export; Z39.50 Client-Server architecture; GUI enabled; multi-tasking; Windows NT/Novell Netware; Finger print device integration and security system, etc. The earlier version though was not compatible with UNOCODE feature; however, the enhanced versions are supporting this standard for coping up with the resources available in bi-directional languages.

Platform

Alice for Windows runs on Windows XP Professional SP2, Windows Server 2003 SP2 (32 Bit) Windows Server 2000 SP4 server platforms. Alice for Windows operates on Windows NT platform. It runs on Windows 98 second edition Windows NT 4.0 Client platform. It, however, does not require RDBMS as it runs on its own database.

Popularity (International Users/Installations)

Its international association has around 17000 installations all around the world and more than 108 offices around the globe. Softlink Asia which markets and promotes Alice for Windows has installations in countries like Sri Lanka, Bangladesh, Maldives, Nepal and Pakistan, etc.

Users (National)

At present, Alice for Windows has about 250 users in India which makes it one of the popular foreign software used by Indian libraries for automating their operations and services. Some of the major Indian libraries using Alice for Windows are: Union Public Service Commission (UPSC), New Delhi; Centre for Environmental Planning and Technology University, Ahmadabad; Central Marine Fisheries Research Institute Cochin, Kerala; Dhirubhai Ambhani International School, Mumbai; Indian Agricultural Statistics Research Institute, New Delhi; Indian Institute of Management (IIM) Ahmadabad; Indian Institute of Petroleum Management (IIPM), Gandhinagar; NIRMA University, Ahmadabad and many more (Softlink Asia, 2013).

SUCHIKA SOFTWARE

Suchika is an Indian born integrated software package for library automation, designed and developed during 1996 by DESIDOC, Delhi for its Defence Science Library and other libraries and Technical Information Centres of Defence Research and Development Organization (DRDO), scattered all across the country. The main purpose of developing this automation package was to help the DRDO research scientists engaged in conducting the research in defence science laboratories by providing services to them at their desktops in an effective and efficient way through automated library system. DESIDOC had also developed one more library automation package namely

Defence Library Management System (DELMS) in 1988 for automating the operations of its library and other libraries of DRDO. Notably, the earlier package i.e. DELMS also had facilities for all housekeeping activities and services.

Modules

Suchika like Granthalaya software package provides the option to install either all modules available in the software at one time, or modular-wise implementation can also be made depending upon the needs and requirements of a particular library. This integrated library management package is available in various modules mentioned hereunder:

- Acquisition
- Cataloguing
- Circulation
- Online Public Access Catalogue (OPAC) and
- Serials control

Besides these modules, Suchkia software also supports online help facilities.

Standards

The package is compatible with international standards like CCF, ISO 2709 and AACR 2 and allows data conversion from Computerized Documentation System/ Integrated Set for Information Systems (CDS/ISIS) developed by UNESCO in 1985 for developing countries. The discussion of CDS/ISIS is given later in this chapter.

Platform

The package has been developed in C^{++} language and is available on MS-DOS and UNIX version platforms keeping in view the requirements of big and small libraries of DRDO. It works on B-tree as data storage technique. In case of DELMS package, it is available on UNIX, Xenix and DOS platforms. The Package has been developed in COBOL programming language with B-tree as data storage technique (Sharma, 1993).

Popularity (Users/Installations)

This package is used by many Indian libraries particularly DESIDOC/DRDO libraries and Technology Information Centres. It's both DOS and UNIX versions have been implemented at Defence Science Library, New Delhi. The developer of Suchika and DELMS i.e. DESIDOC has also decided to offer these packages to non-DRDO libraries at nominal cost to help them in automating their housekeeping operations for modernization and coping up with the modern techno oriented user community to provide them services at their desktops (Saxena & Srivastava, 1998). This package like SOUL and Granthalaya is also cost effective, since it is also indigenous.

MAITREYI SOFTWARE

This package has been developed by Computer Maintenance Corporation of India (CMC) for Calcutta Libraries Network (CALIBNET) with the support of NISSAT. Maitreyi is accredited as the first package which has been developed in India for library network program, providing specific network and communication facilities.

Modules

Maitreyi library automation software package is compatible with the following various modules:

- Acquisition
- Cataloguing
- Circulation
- Online Public Access Catalogue (OPAC) and
- Serials control
- Online help

Standards

The package uses TCP/IP as communication software with X.25 protocol in addition to library management functions.

Platform

The package has been developed on INGRES programming language with Relational database as data storage technique. The software works in UNIX 3.2 operating system and PC-AT 386 as hardware requirement (Saxena & Srivastava, 1998).

Popularity (Users/Installations)

CMC Calcutta is marketing and promoting Maitreyi library software package for automating housekeeping activities and services in Indian libraries. This package is also used by many Indian libraries especially by the libraries which are associated with CALIBNET for automating their operations and services. However, with the development of new integrated library management systems, its use has declined owing to the compatibility of newer packages to international standards and limitations of Maitreyi in supporting these standards.

SANJAY SOFTWARE

DESIDOC has played a very leading role in developing library software packages for automating Indian libraries. Sanjay library software package, like Suchika and DELMS, has also been designed and developed by DESIDOC, Delhi in 1995 with the support of NISSAT, by augmenting CDS/ISIS (Ver 2.3) to cater the needs of Indian library management. The package is comparatively user friendly for housekeeping activities with 70 Pascal's and 25 special menus. Moreover, it has quicker reaction time and efficient interlinking of database.

Modules

Like Maitreyi, Sanjay library package also supports various modules which are mentioned hereunder:

- Acquisition
- Cataloguing
- Circulation
- Online Public Access Catalogue (OPAC)
- Serials control, and
- Online help

Platform

Sanjay version 2.0 operates on MS DOS version 3.2 or above (developed by augmenting CDS/ISIS (Ver 2.3). The package requires PC-AT, 1 MB RAM and 40MB HD as minimum hardware requirement. Further, it has been developed in CDS/ISIS, PASCAL programming language with inverted file as data storage technique.

Popularity (Users/Installations)

The package is marketed by NISSAT, New Delhi at nominal price. Sanjay software has been implemented in many Indian libraries. The package has many installations/users in India, but Technology Bhawan Library and Indian Oil Corporation (IOC) (R&D) libraries, New Delhi are some of the major libraries, where this software is being used (Saxena & Srivastava, 1998). Though Sanjay is low costly package, but it is more likely suitable for small libraries. Consequently, this package is not so widely used especially in larger libraries due to the fact that new integrated packages possess more powerful features and compatibility with international standards as compared to Sanjay software.

VIRTUA SOFTWARE

Virtua is a proprietary Windows based Client-Server fully integrated library management package developed in

1995 by Virginia Technology Library Solutions (VTLS) Inc (now iii innovative). It is the first and leading library automation vendor at Blacksburg, USA. The software is an integrated library system and is acknowledged by more than one thousand eight hundred libraries in forty two countries across the globe. The software is based on six technologies: Relational Database Management System (RDBMS); Rapid development tools; three tier Client Server architecture; database ware housing; UNICODE support and ATM network optimized applications. These technologies facilitate database management handling, software development and network delivery. Virtua supports web OPAC and Chameleon iportal that facilitates users to interact with the library by enabling them to share the material that they have seen or observed on different popular social networking sites like Twitter, Facebook, etc.

Modules

Virtua has achieved global recognition by virtue of its robust features and standard modules. The software is versatile with following modules:

- Acquisition and Fund Accounting
- Cataloguing
- Circulation
- Serials control
- Online Public Access Catalogue (OPAC)
- Statistics and Reporting
- Chameleon Gateway.

Standards

VTLS, the developer of Virtua, realized the importance of other major languages of the world; therefore, it designed Virtua to provide robust foreign language capabilities with UNICODE standard to facilitate data entry in multiple languages. Virtua software is credited as the first software in library automation industry to have coined the compatibility with UNICODE standard. This leading software supports all formats. It accommodates different versions of MARC standards such as USMARC; UKMARC; CANMARC; SEWMARC; etc. and is also compatible with MARC 21 format. Besides above, Virtua supports ANSI/ISO Z39.50, MARC21, ISO-23950, ISO-10161 standards. It also fully supports RDA and FRBR standards which almost all of the Indian packages and most of the international packages falls short of. It is compatible with TCP/IP communication protocol and possesses windows GUI as profiler. The UNICODE feature of Virtua also supports data entry in Urdu, Arabic and Persian languages.

Platform

Virtua is a Windows based Client-Server architecture. The software operates on UNIX and Linux operating systems and uses Oracle Relational Database Management System (RDBMS) at its backend. Virtua operates on UNIX, LINUX, SOLARIS, SUSE LINUX, IBM(AIX), SUN(SOLARIS) server platforms with 95/98/2000/NT/XP/Vista, Linux as Client platforms.

Popularity (Users/Installations)

Although Virtua is one of the leading library management software in the world; however, because of its non-cost effectiveness particularly for developing countries, it is not as widely used in Indian libraries as the earlier discussed softwares. Nevertheless, its robust standards and features attract large libraries across the globe to install this package for automating their operations. Subsequently, some about 40 Indian libraries including National Library, Kolkata; Jawaharlal Nehru University (JNU), New Delhi; Central Institute of Indian Languages, Mysore, IIT Madras, Indian Institute of Science and Education Research (IISER), Kolkata; Indian Institute of

Management, Ranchi; Indian Institute of Management, Bangalore; Indian Institute of Technology, Bhubaneswar and University of Kashmir, Srinagar are presently some of the prominent Indian libraries using Virtua software for better and efficient automation of their operations and services (VTLS, 2012). It is worth mentioning here that the number of large Indian libraries presently switching over to this leading international integrated library management system is growing at a very fast rate.

LIBRIS SOFTWARE

LIBRIS is a comprehensive library management system developed by Frontier Information Technology Private Limited based at Secunderabad, India for optimizing the utilization of library facilities by members and management of library functions by the library staff.

Modules

This package consists of following main modules, besides some additional facilities like that of Suchika and Sanjay softwares:

- Acquisition
- Cataloguing
- Circulation and
- Serials control

Standards and Platform

LIBRIS is available on INGRES, 'C' languages with relational database as data storage technique. It can be used in single-user version on MS-DOS platform, while as on multi-user version; it can be used on UNIX platform. This package also supports bar coding facility for easier circulation activities.

Popularity (Users/Installations)

LIBRIS software package is used by many Indian libraries; however, State Bank College, Jawaharlal Nehru

Technological University, India International Centre, Physical Research Laboratory, Sri Venkiteswara Central library and Electronics Corporation of India Limited are some of the major institutions that have used LIBRIS package for their library automation (Ravikumar, 1995). However, presently there is a growing trend among Indian libraries towards using more powerful integrated library management systems packed with compatibility to international standards.

TULIPS SOFTWARE

Tata Unisys Library Information Processing System (TULIPS) is a comprehensive library management package developed at TUL Bangalore Centre for better and faster information dissemination to users as well as computerization of certain housekeeping activities of libraries. Since its inception, this package has brought many enhanced versions such as 4.6.0., 4.6.1 and 4.6.7 etc. to cope up with the emerging and heterogeneous needs of libraries. However, barring some technological institutions of Karnataka State of Indian union, this package is very less used by large Indian libraries.

Modules

The modular wise details of TULIPS package is given hereunder:

- Acquisition control
- Cataloguing
- Circulation
- Serials control and
- Utilities

Platform

TULIPS software package is developed under Oracle and uses RDBMS. The package operates on UNIX platform.

Popularity (Users/Installations)

This package is also used in some Indian libraries for automating their library system. American Studies Research Centre, Hyderabad and Ramakrishna Institute of Culture, Calcutta had also installed this system (Ranjan, 1995). Baring some libraries especially in Bangalore, this package is not presently used as widely as the other above discussed packages in Indian libraries.

LIBRARIAN SOFTWARE

This library management software package is a codeless library management package developed by Soft-Aid, Pune. It is a menu driven and user friendly software used by persons having little or no previous background of computers. This package like previous ones has also brought many enhanced versions such as web Librarian, New Librarian XI and Cyberarian for better handling of all housekeeping operations.

Modules

Librarian software package is available with following modules:

- Cataloguing
- Circulation
- Serials control
- Acquisition
- Budget control, and
- Bibliographic services.

The software also possesses article indexing, barcode generation and member ID generation facilities.

Standards

The Librarian management software package is able to cope up with the needs of all types of libraries and is compatible with most of the international standards like MARC21; AACR2 Z39.50 and NCIP 2.0. In case of webLibrarian version, it is also compatible to international standards such as AACR 2; MARC21; MARCXML; Z39.50; NCIP 2.0 and UNICODE feature. While as New Librarian XI version based on NET 2.0 framework supports NCIP 2.0 for RFID; Z39.50; MARC 21 for import/export; extensive and customized web OPAC; UNICODE; web interface and multimedia resource management features (CR2 Knowledge World, 2014).

Platform

Librarian package operates on DOS (Ver 3.2) and above in single-user mode. While as multi-user mode operates on Xenix and Novell Network platforms (Ravikumar, 1995). It supports LAN and requires PC-AT 386 as hardware requirement like Maitreyi software. Librarian software complies all the requirements of National Accreditation and Assessment Centre (NAAC)/ All India Council of Technical Education (AICTE) agencies.

Popularity (Users/Installations)

The use of webLibrarian and Cyberarian versions of Librarian automation package is rarely seen in Indian libraries, but the original Librarian package was used by some libraries earlier.

WINISIS SOFTWARE

WINISIS is a Windows version of Computerized Documentation System/Integrated Set for Information Systems (CDS/ISIS) developed specially for school libraries by UNSECO in 1985. It is information storage and retrieval software developed by UNESCO to satisfy the needs of many institutions, especially in developing countries. The software supports three languages: English, Arabic and French. The software needs no conversion when moving from CDS/ISIS DOS to CDS/ISIS for Windows. The software is installed on stand-alone mode. This software also had some enhanced versions, but their usage declined sharply with the advent of more versatile integrated library management packages. Its latest official versions include WINISIS 1.5 build 3 (Standard) and WINISIS 1.5 build 7 (Arabic enabled).

Standards

WINISIS is compatible with all Windows operating systems. However, Windows NT/2000/XP users should read the troubleshooting section of the "readme" file installed by the WINISIS installation program (UNESCO, 2011). Data interchange function is based on the ISO 2709 international standard used by leading database producers. CDS/ISIS for windows (WINISIS) fully supports MARC 21 format, it requires Windows 3.1 or higher as operating system with 4MB hard disk, 8 MB RAM, CPU 486 Processer at 40Mhz and Floppy and CD-ROM Drive with colour screen monitor and printer (CDS/ISIS for Windows WINISIS, n. d.).

Popularity (Users/Installations)

Though the earlier versions of this software were MS-DOS based, but still it was used in many small libraries and corporate libraries, as well as some sections of large academic libraries in India for automating some of their operations. However, due to the availability of standard integrated library management software in Indian market, a very few libraries are still using WINISIS. Some libraries of developing countries including India, Pakistan, Nepal, Sri Lanka and some Arabian countries still use this package, though integrated library management systems have better features and standards with compatibility to international standards.

MINISIS SOFTWARE

This package developed by International development research centre, Ottava Canada is also a good package for library work.

Modules

MINISIS software package supports following modules:

- Cataloguing
- Circulation
- Serials control
- Report generation

It also provides interfaces to remote online information systems.

Standards and Platform

MINISIS supports ISO 2709 international standard for data interchange. It is compatible with UNIMARC format and also supports standard databases like AGRIS, DEVSIS etc. MINISIS package requires Huerlett-Packard system programming language (SPL) and runs on HP-3000 mini-computers with the requirement of 512 KB memory.

Popularity (Users/Installations)

MINISIS was used by about 200 libraries till the fall of 2000 A.D. in India. During that period India Central Secretariat Library; New Delhi Library, Calcutta; National Informatics Centre and Indira Ghandi National Centre or Arts etc. were some of the major users of MINISIS package (Vasanth & Mahesh, 2000). However, due to the emergence of standard integrated library management software in Indian market, a very few libraries are presently using WINISIS package.

Besides the above discussed softwares, there are a number of other library packages available in Indian market. To mention a few, Archive 1,2,3; Basisplus and Techlibplus; Catman; Libman; Libra; Library manager; Lib Soft; List plus; Loan Soft, Nirmals; Salim; Trishna; Ulysis; Wilisys, PALMS; Troodon and Tulib etc. are some of the packages used by some libraries in the past, however, their usage almost declined to naught in the present era of robust integrated library management systems.

Based on the fact that some leading indigenous and international integrated library packages have been discussed in detail with respect to their relevant modules and features and their installations in leading libraries in India and abroad, it is hoped that this book will pave a way for Indian librarians in selecting the appropriate standard integrated library system for fully automating Indian library system.

REFERENCES

CDS/ISIS for Windows WINISIS. (n.d.) Retrieved January 13, 2015 from http://www.alibnet.org/public/bookofpaper/ppts/32.pdf.

CR2 Knowledge World. (2014). *Products.* Retrieved January 13, 2015 from http://www.cr2.in/products/products-library.html

e-Granthalaya. (2015). *Homepage.* Retrieved January 13, 2015 from http://egranthalaya.nic.in/Default.aspx

INFLIBNET (2014). *Software for University Libraries about SOUL 2.0,* Retrieved Feb 13, 2014 from http://www.inflibnet.ac.in/soul/about.html

LibSys Corporation. (2012). *Homepage.* Retrieved Feb 23, 2013 from http://www.LibSys.co.in/home.html

Ranjan, V. (1995). Information Trends in Library for Computer Professionals. In Nair Raman R (Ed.)., *Academic Library Automation* (p. 102). New Delhi: ESS ESS.

Ravikumar, S. R. (1995). Software Packages for Academic Library System. In Nair Raman R. (Ed.)., *Academic Library Automation* (pp. 138-148). New Delhi: ESS ESS.

Saxena, SC., & Srivastava, R. K. (1998). Evaluation of Library Software Packages Available in India. *DESIDOÇ Bulletin of Information Technology,* 18(5), 11-13. Retrieved August 3, 2015 from http://publications.drdo.gov.in

Sharma, P. S. K. (1993). *Library Computerization Theory & Practice.* New Delhi: ESS ESS, pp. 103-144.

Softlink Asia. (2013). *Homepage.* Retrieved Feb 25, 2013 from http://www.softlinkasia.com/index.html

SOUL 2.0 State-of-the-art integrated library management software. (2014). *Homepage.* Retrieved Feb 25, 2014 from http://www.inflibnet.ac.in/soul/

Vasanth, N., & Mudhol, M. V. (2000). *Software packages for Library Automation.* New Delhi: ESS ESS, p. 66.

VTLS. (2012). *Products.* Retrieved March 9, 2012 from http://www.vtls.com/products/virtua

UNESCO. (2011). *CDS/ISIS for Windows.* Retrieved July 11, 2015 from http://portal.unesco.org/ci/en/ev.php-URL_ID=5330&URL_DO=DO_TOPIC&UR L_SECTION=201.html#intro

4

Automating Housekeeping Operations

This chapter discusses about the different housekeeping operations that call for automation in accordance with their vitality and coherence. Further, these operations and services have been discussed in relevance to their effectiveness and usage. Moreover, the chapter thoroughly throws light on different modules of popularly used library management systems in Indian libraries with their relevance to the features and functions available in these packages.

BACKGROUND

Indian Library automation has developed significantly with the availability of a number of indigenous and international library management systems in Indian market for automating housekeeping operations of college and university libraries. However, the selection of appropriate software package for implementing an effective integrated library system, which would cater to the needs of both libraries and their users, has been a challenging task for Indian librarians. Although a number of indigenous library softwares primarily developed by research and development organizations have served Indian libraries for long, but only few of them survived, while the rest did not last long majorly because of their incompatibility with international standards.

Owing to these incompatibility issues and robust features of integrated library management systems, many Indian libraries switched over to international software packages to overcome these drawbacks. In this direction, the libraries, particularly those associated with research and development centers and reputed Indian universities started using standard library management softwares to enhance their operations and services. Though, it is discouraging to note that the conditions of services and operations of most of the academic libraries in India have been unsatisfactory. However during the last two decades, the college and university libraries of India with the financial support of UGC along with the landmark development of INFLIBNET (an inter-university centre of UGC) gained the significant momentum for automating their library system. These initiatives coupled with the development of SOUL software by INFLIBNET played a key role to enhance the efficiency and effectiveness of Indian academic libraries in an automated era. Needless, to note here that further development is required to improve the present state of automated library system of Indian libraries with special reference to the libraries of developing Indian States including Uttar Pradesh, Madhya Pradesh, Assam, Bihar, Rajasthan, North Eastern Sates and Jammu and Kashmir, etc. for effective utilization of their valuable resources.

GENERAL FEATURES OF LIBRARY AUTOMATION

Before planning for automation project in libraries, many general features shall be given prior considerations. These features include hardware requirements, cost of the software, operating systems, programming language, quality of the software, data searching and retrieval techniques, flexibility for accommodating enhanced versions, user friendliness of OPAC, better interface, import/export facility and more importantly the compatibility with international standards. Different leading library management packages shall be thoroughly evaluated with these features in prior consideration, before implementing a particular package for automation. However, budget shall not be now a major bottleneck, as viewed earlier, for procuring standard library management package, since adequate grants are now provided by UGC and INFLIBNET for automating college and university libraries in India.

In the perspective of automation in libraries, the majority of academic libraries in India fall short to modernize their operations and services, though some libraries have done substantial amount of work for automating their housekeeping operations.

In case of operating systems, Linux as a server platform with any version of Windows as a Client is being regarded as most suitable operating system for library environment. The reason for this is that the Linux has stronger database security than other operating systems and the menace of virus is unheard of in the Linux world. In turn, it helps to save extra expenses on buying anti viruses to protect the database. The cost factor is another obvious advantage of Linux as it is freely available. The best part of Linux is that it is open source. It means besides getting it free of charge, users will be able to modify the source code to suit their desires by adding more features or removing undesired ones.

Regarding compatibility with international standards, library management package should be able to support standard ISO 2709 for data exchange, entry in USMARC, CANMARC and UKMARC etc., besides being compatible with UNICODE standard for supporting entry in bi-directional/multi-lingual scripts. These standards help in preserving the original language of resources. Significantly, these resources are displayed in OPAC in their original script. The new technology viz Radio Frequency Identification (RFID) technology compatibility shall also be given prior thought, before selecting the software package for automation.

SUPPORT SERVICES OF THE LIBRARY MANAGEMENT SYSTEMS

As far as services of the vendors of the softwares are concerned, it should be chalked out in detail at the planning stage. The vendor support system is also prior consideration in automation project. Besides discussing Annual Maintenance Contract (AMC) with the vendors, the libraries which plan to automate its housekeeping operations shall also discuss the onsite and offsite training by vendors. However, a thorough modular wise training program will be appropriate for librarians to achieve the advantages of all the features available in a particular package. It may be stated here that vendor performance has always been a bottleneck in utilizing the available features to its full extent.

HOUSEKEEPING OPERATIONS

Technology has had and will probably continue to have a remarkable impact on housekeeping operations and other services of any kind of library. It is the key force for changing the core work culture of any kind of library situation. Owing to the fact that contemporary libraries are indeed required to justify their existence and satisfy the expectations of their techno-oriented users by providing them their desired information at their desktops in the present technology driven world, this tendency of technology will unquestionably find its way into large academic and research libraries set up in any country.

Even though the library automation practically took off in India in 1970s, however, it has been only during the last two decades as stated earlier that Indian academic libraries have gained significant momentum in automating their housekeeping operations and other services. Presently, a large number of Indian libraries attached with universities, IITs and research centers are implementing integrated library systems for effectively automating their library system. Nevertheless, due to the late arrival of technology in India chiefly because of its developing economy, the library staff and user community with special mention of academic universities still possess limited technological knowledge in effectively managing automated library system. Therefore, the implications of this study and the studies alike for technological changes and improvements in academic libraries still hold their validity to help out Indian librarians for successfully automating their library system, though the libraries of developed countries have been doing so since long.

Broadly speaking the areas of library automation commonly called as housekeeping operations are classified into following divisions or operations:

- Acquisition
- Cataloguing
- Circulation
- Serials control
- Article indexing and
- OPAC

All these operations have been discussed and debated in the following pages.

AUTOMATING ACQUISITION

The different modules with the status of their relevant features have been discussed into following different tables:

Table 2. Acquisition Module

S.No.	*Features*
1	Shall Enable faster pre-order duplicate checking.
2	Enable to keep up-to-date vendor database.
3	Facilitate easy preparation of purchase orders.
4	Facilitates downloading of bibliographic data from CD-ROMS, international databases like LC, OCLC, RLIN, WLN, etc. or vendor supplied electronic catalogues.
5	Enables electronic ordering and easy book selection.
6	Follows the Goods Offices Committee (GOC) conversion rates.
7	Manages the budget and shows the status of budget, before the order is placed.
8	Facilitates to purchase the books in demand and keep the remaining books in pending.
9	Permits modification in discount rates.
10	Accepts the books in gift/exchange or gratis.
11	Facilitate to send timely reminders and letters for cancellation of supply orders.
12	Enable to maintain up to date fund utilization account.
13	Facilitates easy accessioning and invoice processing.
14	Helps in preparation of vendor performance report.
15	Facilitate prompt notification to users.
16	Facilitate to send letters to banks for foreign exchange drafts.
17	Software allows the library staff to generate customized reports.

Acquisition is the core activity in any library which requires sound knowledge of librarianship. In manual acquisition, difficulties in monitoring growing collections, preparing and updating supplier list, sending reminders and management of budget are a common place. In automated libraries, librarians can found a complete solution to these problems in an automated acquisition system. It is a unanimous revelation that librarians have never imagined that their task would be so simple with the help of library automation software. This opinion also substantiates one of earlier studies conducted by (Rajgopalan, 1981).

An automated library system uses the power and advantages of computer facility to improve the various processes involved in acquisition. Reynolds briefly compared both manual and automated systems as follows:

"Manual acquisition systems are extremely labor intensive as well as paper intensive and usually allow for only a limited range of management information to be compiled. Automated acquisition system, on the other hand, can substantially reduce the amount of paper shuffling and can perform a number of monitoring activities and generate reports that escape manual systems" (Reynolds, 1985).

Based on the above, it would be pertinent to mention here that in manual acquisition section, the most tedious job is duplicate checking. However, this can be performed with much ease in an automated acquisition system. There is requirement for selected materials to be checked in pre-order, on-order, in process and already catalogued materials. Such provisions are better handled separately in automated acquisition system. Pertinently, all the standard library management packages provide this facility.

In a manual system, the libraries use to prepare manual records of all the vendors. Sometimes, the updation of these records uses to consume too much time. On contrary in an automated system, editing of any record is quite simple. Consequently, this feature in acquisition module has made the otherwise tedious job easier and accurate. The purchase orders which otherwise in manual system were prolonged and error prone have now become error free, besides saving a lot of mental and manual effort in automated acquisition system. In case of vendor database, the updation is done as per the requirements of a particular library. The librarians are now handling these operations with joy as these available features have made editing quite simpler.

When a library desires to acquire any book, the first step in that direction would be to enter the data either directly into the system or imported from some external sources such as databases like LC, OCLC, RLIN, WLN, etc. into its files. Although, acquisition system enables electronic ordering and easy book selection facilities as mentioned earlier. However, it depends on the technical and professional expertise of librarians to use such facilities. It may be mentioned here that there may be handful of libraries in India which are using these facilities to their fullest. It is also important to mention here that automated system supports different modes of acquisition such as firm orders, on-approval, on exchange solicited gift items.

Furthermore, once a decision to purchase any publication is taken by the library, the order should be procured and sent to vendors, publishers depending on the mode of acquisition for each of the items that are ready for purchase. All these activities are carried out in automated acquisition module accurately. The usage of international databases as mentioned above for importing bibliographic data from external sources is another beauty of automated acquisition system. But disappointingly barring some libraries, these facilities and features remains to be seen in Indian academic libraries. This may owe to the fact that Indian librarians largely require the desired level of training from the vendor and efficiency in using the external bibliographic data.

Another advantage of automated acquisition system is the reminders which are sent within a fraction of minute to as many as desired number of users. These reminders in manual system were so prolonged that they become irrelevant on reaching to their destination. Similarly letters for claiming or cancellation of orders is also fast and accurate in automated acquisition. Moreover, amending or cancelling orders which were delayed and expensive in manual system are now possible to be fast and cheap. Notably this feature helps in fast, effective and efficient control over ordering, claiming and cancellation activities. Although sending hard copies as reminders have become irrelevant now in automated acquisition system, however, most of Indian libraries still continue with this practice. In case any vendor fails to supply the desired materials within the framed time period, there should be provision of cancelling both full and part of the supply order in the acquisition module.

A significant feature in an acquisition system is the management of allocated budgets and the preparation of financial statements. Notably, the allocation of funds is done in the beginning of fiscal year; nevertheless, it could be re-allocated anytime during the financial year. An automated acquisition system should be capable to handle all the budgetary functions. Taking the advantage of available features, some notable university libraries in India are maintaining their different budget heads using the available features in the acquisition module of the respective softwares. It is worthy to mention here that the acquisition librarians' of these libraries feels happy with these features, because in the manual procedure lot of calculations were needed to be done. Furthermore, there were always chances of human errors in the mathematical calculations.

Maintenance of budget is the keystone of acquisition section. Indian librarians were quite disappointed with respect to management of budgets in manual methods. Now, in an automated environment, transfer of funds between different heads of budget is possible. The librarians feel now happiness that there is least probability in committing errors as far as calculation is concerned. In a lighter mode, it can be stated that those librarians who are very weak in arithmetic's and are errors prone in the manual calculations are now satisfied with automated acquisitions. Furthermore, the librarians are also quite happy with the feature that contains a log of transactions affecting accounts which can be printed out by date and item as well as by any account operator. This revelation also validate the results shown in the study of (Harrison and Summers, 1988) related to acquisition section of the Lancaster Library.

When an ordered item is received, it is important that all the functions associated with receipts like invoice processing and payments are done to enable the processing of further steps in order to make the item available before the user community. According to Reynolds, given below are some of the useful receiving functions.

On receipt of an item, automatic notification should be generated by the system, if the actual price exceeds the encumbered price by a specified percentage. On receipt, the system should immediately update all files including fund accounts, display of system-supplied instructions or options disposition of items (Reynolds, 1985).

Regarding received item processing, the function is straightforward i.e. the item is received along with an invoice. The librarians enter the details of invoice, copies supplied, cost price of the item, currency in which the cost is invoiced, etc., this is done in order to facilitate the further steps such as accessioning and invoice processing. Nevertheless, there are some issues particularly in case of conversion of foreign currency rates. Apparently, this difference owes to the library management software. In this case, such issues in the software shall be tuned before hand to fix this problem.

The vendor performance report shows how effective the service of a particular vendor has been. The report can show the supplies that the vendor has been able to make within different time intervals like 1-15 days, 16-31 days, etc., and the ratio of number of books supplied to the number ordered in a given period of time. The acquisition module of all standard library management packages help in the preparation of vendor performance report. Notably, many Indian libraries have been using this facility fully, though they also maintain manual register of vendors. Pertinently, this feature enables to produce comparative analysis of different vendors. It helps to know the status and reputation of a particular vendor in supplying the orders timely.

Goods Office Committee (GOC) conversion rates, modification in discount rates, acceptance of books in gifts/gratis and displaying the status of budget before placing the order are other wonderful benefits of automating acquisition system, however, there would be rarely any library in India using these features of automated acquisition system. This may largely be because Indian librarians have not still gained that much technical efficiency in using these features. Nevertheless, conversion rates are now-a-days easier to carry out by the help of online facility. Though some libraries are doing customization of discount rates, but it is not done to a satisfactory level.

The automated acquisition system facilitates to send letters to banks for foreign exchange drafts; exchange rates; unit prices; discounts: currencies, etc. However, majority of Indian libraries are yet to realize the wonderful benefits of this facility. Pertinently, this feature helps to speed up the transactions through online payments which is a common practice in the libraries of developed world.

All the standard library management packages have the capability to send prompt notification to users. These packages facilitate sending user notification through SMS and e-mail. While some packages like Virtua integrated library management software send prompt alert to users through Really Simple Syndicate (RSS) updates. Users can subscribe to RSS feed of frequently changing content in Chamo social OPAC. It may be mentioned here that the Chamo OPAC is an enhanced version of OPAC. It is more interactive and user friendly than OPAC. By subscribing, users will receive updates via text messages or e-mails. Unfortunately SMS facility is not been practiced to its full extent as is being done in the libraries of America, UK, Germany, Australia, etc. This facility lets the staff to quickly inform patrons about the status of their requested titles. It helps to keep the users updated of new acquisitions that are related to their field of study. It is worth mentioning here that some libraries send notification to users about new titles through e-mail that is maintained in the users' profile, while some displays the flash news of new acquisitions in the OPAC of the library.

In addition to above, the automated acquisition should also be able to generate vendor wise report and department wise report. These reports are normally generated for details of expenditure showing budget allocated, budget paid and commitment and balance budget. In case of vendor wise report, they are generated for a desired fiscal year and for a desired vendor. Likewise, departmental reports are also generated for a desired fiscal year and for a desired department. Besides these, automated acquisition shall also generate reports like:

- Indents/Requisitions
- Documents on approval
- Recommended and non recommended indents
- Pending Indents
- Vendor wise indents
- Receipt
- Acquired documents
- Vendor list
- Vendor wise orders

- Accession Register
- Catalogue cards
- List of additions, etc.

The acquisition module of standard integrated library management systems usually provides such facilities. However in using maximum features of automated acquisition, the librarians of IITs are more versatile than the librarians of academic libraries. This difference in the usage is because of the fact that the library staff of IITs gain more knowledge of acquisition module through self training or hit and trial method. They try it, because, they are confident that if their system goes down, it will be fixed swiftly due to their techno savvy nature. On contrary, the library staff of academic libraries is not so much confident in trial methods, and therefore, lags behind in using all the features of acquisition module to its full extent. This is also the general realization that acquisition is the first stage of automation process, and if any library fails to automate acquisition section effectively, the entire project of automation will come to standstill.

AUTOMATING CATALOGUING

After acquisition, the onus directly comes on the staff of cataloguing section to keep the book ready for circulation for its ultimate use. In a traditional library, cataloguers were facing a lot of problems in the whole cataloguing process, because of lacking of standardization. One of the attractive benefits of automating cataloguing section in libraries is the standardization. Appreciably, many Indian libraries with special mention of those attached with research and development and technological institutions have gained significant achievement as they almost converted all their records into MARC 21 format. On the other hand, academic libraries are little less interested in some international standards, though some libraries are not behind. The chief reason for this disparity is that the special libraries' staff is keeping themselves abreast with the latest developments in the field of software packages and other application softwares. Pertinently, their staff achieves this level of efficiency by attending various workshops and conferences. In case of academic libraries as stated earlier, the standardization is yet to be achieved fully.

Cataloguing is one of the most vital housekeeping operations of libraries that call for automation at first. The automation of this operation requires much professional and technical efficiency from librarians' for its effective usage by end users. The automation of this operation shall positively comprise the following features:

Table 3. Cataloguing Module

S.No.	*Features*
1	Creation of record of a document only once, easy cataloguing.
2	Elimination of repetitive work.
3	The cataloguing module shall support easy and MARC based data entry.
4	Enables import and export of data in international formats like MARC/CCF(ISO 2709) /MARC21.
5	Helpful to do easy copy cataloguing like downloading catalogue records from external bibliographic databases such as OCLC, LC, etc.
6	Cataloguing module supports international standards.
7	Standards such as FRBR, RDA, RFID shall be available.
8	Shall make full use of UNICODE feature.
9	Shall be able to support in compiling of Union Catalogues.
10	Able to support centralized cataloguing of resources.
11	Shall provide many access points and in-depth subject cataloguing.
12	Searchability by any field.
13	Automating cataloguing shall generate and maintain authority files.
14	Prepare shelf list and index files.
15	Produces Spine and Bar code labels.

16 Enable the maintenance of thesaurus and availability of dictionary for entering data and select terms.

17 Enable the library staff in cataloguing module and users in OPAC to customize the output reports in any desired format.

Automation of cataloguing in libraries involves the preparation of a record which can be read by a machine and also by human beings. This record is prepared only once by the cataloguer; the input of that record into computer is done with the help of either data entry operator or library staff. Automated cataloguing thus eliminates repetitive work involved in manual cataloguing. More so, there is no requirement of added entries in automated cataloguing. The most compelling reason to automate the cataloguing function of a library is to make the catalogue available for public access and also to remote users with the help of internet. Mentioning the advantages of automated cataloguing system, Woods stated that in manual system, all cards have to be drafted, checked, proof read, corrected, sorted and filed. If any book is moved to a new location, weeded out or manipulated, all the cards will have to be fixed out and corrected accordingly. On contrary in a computer based system, file needs only one amendment to correct all the entries, besides having various other advantages (Woods, 1986).

Having realized these advantages of an automated cataloguing system, majority of large Indian university libraries have been using most of the available features of cataloguing modules of their respective softwares. These features have proved very helpful and contributed in many ways to bring efficiency and effectiveness in the entire library system. Significant advantages have been discussed hereunder:

Automating cataloguing has made the process of cataloguing easier with the help of standard integrated library management packages. It is worth mentioning here that before the application of related features of automated cataloguing, potential users had to wait around four weeks to get newly acquired material. However, this time lag has now been shortened considerably. Now the book in automated cataloguing is made available in shorter period of time as compared to that of earlier manual systems.

Cataloguing and its associated processes like classification and subject indexing are among the most cost-intensive processes in a library. In a developed nation like USA, the cost of original cataloguing ranges between 25-30 dollars per book, though it is not that much costly in India (Haravua, 2004). It has been a common opinion now that automation has played a significant role in reducing the cost of cataloguing books. This has been largely possible with the help of sharing catalogue records over networks and also by using MARC data from library networks such as INFLIBNET and Developing Library Network (DELNET) in India. It is pertinent to state here that the large Indian academic libraries are either a member of INFLIBNET or DELNET or both, besides being the member of various other networks in India.

One of the most important reasons for automation of cataloguing section is to achieve standardization as stated earlier. In this direction, all the major libraries of India have made significant achievements and converted almost all their records in MARC21 format. However, some resources available in less spoken Indian languages and difficult to enter into the respective softwares have not been converted into MARC 21 format till date. These resources are notably being kept as rare and reserve collection in the Indian libraries.

Apart from the above mentioned benefits, standard library management packages as discussed in chapter-3 are used for downloading of some cataloguing records from important bibliographic databases. However, it remains to be seen that to what extent this wonderful feature of automated cataloguing is being used by Indian libraries.

It may be mentioned here that most of the Indian libraries were earlier using either In-house software or indigenous software for automating cataloguing system. But with their limitations in import and export data exchange facility, many libraries switched over to standard foreign integrated library management packages. Thus importing the data from international softwares with the help of import/export facility available in modern software packages became possible.

Automation has greatly influenced the cataloguing division or technical section of libraries. The impact has been far reaching and profound in the technical sections of Indian libraries. In this respect, import and export facilities was grossly missing in the earlier Indian library management packages and librarians were facing harsh experience with regard to importing the data from one software to other. But with the availability and implementation of enhanced version of Indian and international library softwares such as LibSys, Virtua, Alice for Windows software etc., the data import has been found smooth and hassle free. However, the reality cannot be escaped as the whole process of import and export of data in Indian libraries is mostly done in the presence of representatives' of particular vendors. This suggests that the import/export feature in the software should always be done in presence of representative of the library software vendors.

Though a large number of Indian libraries have implemented automation, however, none of the libraries including those which are considered as champions in library automation such as IIT libraries, Aligarh Muslim University, Jamia Millia Islamia, Jawaharlal Nehru University, Ranbaxy, Torment Pharmaceutical Company, etc., have become the members of OCLC. They seem to be unaware about the fact that to what extent, the membership of OCLC will benefit the staff of cataloguing division. It is worth noting here that some libraries such as Central Library, IIT Delhi, Central Library, Jawaharlal University, Allama Iqbal Library, Kashmir University, etc., have become the members of OCLC. The libraries which are members of OCLC joyously use copy cataloguing utility through OCLC database that has made cataloguing very economical. This finding substantiates the study conducted by (Hirshon, 1988) related to OCLC services. Needless to mention that cataloguing, classification and subject indexing are very costly in non OCLC member libraries in India. In view of the number of benefits of OCLC membership mentioned above, Indian university libraries shall at an earliest register with OCLC to ease the burden of cataloging. The same is applicable to all other large libraries which are yet away from the benefits of OCLC membership.

Compatibility to all international standards was the major bottleneck of most of the indigenous library softwares. Owing majorly to this drawback, some reputed Indian libraries migrated to foreign softwares to support all international standards. However, the standards such as RDA, FRBR and RFID are yet to be operational in most of the libraries. Though some libraries are pooling their efforts for standardization, it is, however, foresighted that in near future most of the large Indian libraries will install latest versions of their respective softwares or will implement standard integrated library management systems for achieving standardization by using such standards. It may also be pointed out here that some libraries are doing wonders by making use of standard systems like self check-in/out stations for transaction of their resources and RFID based sensor gates to check the mischievous users. Notably, the availability of book drop boxes at different points in the library and foresightedly in hostels have altogether lessened the burden of circulation desk. Regarding RDA and FRBR standards, only few libraries are using these features. It apparently seems that the librarians require more time, training and efficiency in using these standards which could overcome the burden of circulation and other processes. The book drop boxes for self return of library books and RFID sensor gates for eradicating book theft in modern libraries have been shown diagrammatically hereunder.

Fig. 18 Diagrammatic representation of Library User using RFID Smart Card to open the Library Gate

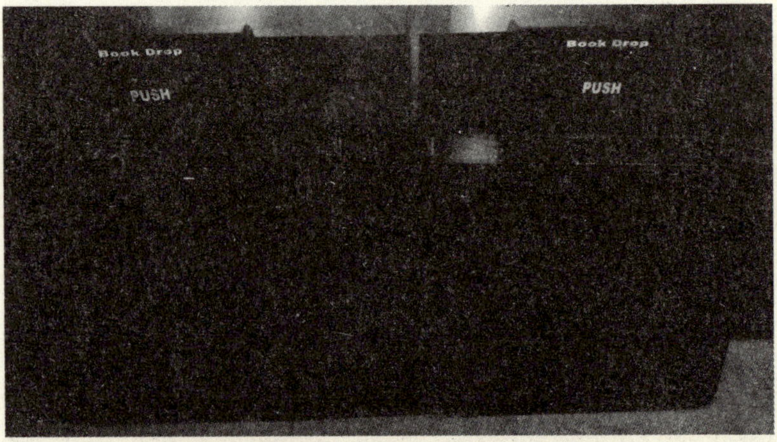

Fig. 19. Diagrammatic display of Book Drop Boxes in Modern Libraries

UNICODE standard for the input, storage and retrieval of bibliographic data in multiple languages is one of the robust features of automated cataloguing available in standard library packages. This feature primarily lets the librarians to preserve the resources available in Hindi, Arabic, Persian, Urdu and other bi-directional languages in their own scripts. Moreover, their retrieval on OPAC is also done in the same script. But, disappointingly not many Indian libraries have till date given the desired preference for the creation of database using UNICODE feature of the standard library management packages. It is seen that the UNICODE standard of Virtua library software package as against Indian packages is more effective.

Though standardization shall be given prior consideration before the implementation, but the compatibility with standards like UNICODE, FRBR, RDA, etc., because of their wonderful benefits in cataloguing as achieved by the American and British libraries are suggested to be checked, before installing a particular package. In this direction, UGC and INFLIBNET in collaboration with National Library at Kolkata can play a pivotal role in making standardization mandatory for enhancing the utilization and effectiveness of library operations and services of college and university libraries in India.

Retrospective conversion as suggested from above paras shall be discussed in detail before undertaking the automation project. Though most of the automated libraries in India have undergone for retrospective conversion of their collection, but there are enough apprehensions that there would be any Indian academic library which may have fully completed retrospective conversion. The reason to this issue lies in the fact that many libraries have kept a large collection under reserved category. It may be stated here that retrospective conversion is the process of turning the existing paper catalogue records of library into machine readable form.

Another beauty of library automation is centralized cataloguing, in which all the resources acquired within a system of branch/departmental libraries are undertaken by central library, so that the results of such cataloguing are used by departmental/branch libraries also. Pertinently, centralized cataloguing largely helps to evade the duplication of titles, saves the manpower consumed in cataloguing by branch libraries and maintains uniformity in standards and elements of data entry. Unfortunately, less number of Indian libraries as that of Western libraries makes use of centralized cataloguing feature available in standard packages, while as some few are partially doing centralized cataloguing.

Compiling Union Catalogue has been a challenging task for Indian librarians since long, but the availability of enhanced version of standard Indian library packages and installation of foreign softwares has provided a long sought solution to this problem. There are many standard library management systems which have the capacity to link the Union catalogues online. The Z39.50 complaint feature of LibSys for instance makes networking of libraries more effective and promotes resource sharing in a networked environment. On contrary, the multiple settings make links to Union catalogue a simple process in Virtua- another standard foreign library management package. Users can insert library symbols into bibliographic records to track record ownership of other libraries in network. However, it is disappointing to note that hardly any Indian academic library is using Union catalogue feature of their respective softwares, though IITs being techno savvy. The reason may largely be because that very few Indian libraries have formal agreement of resource sharing with other libraries, but at the same time some notable libraries like that of IITs, IIMs and central universities share some of their resources within the ambit of well established IITs and central universities in India only.

Very few efforts have been taken for compiling Union catalogues in India, a union catalogue of all the established IITs and central universities is recommended here. It is worth mentioning here that such a Union catalogue will greatly help in reducing the cost incurred on collection development for the newly established IITs and other technical institutions and central universities across the country. It will also help college and university libraries in India in procuring up-to-date and vibrant collection.

A wonderful advantage of automated cataloguing is the facility of many access points and support to in-depth subject cataloguing. It enables to prepare many entries such as title; subject; author; call No.; ISBN; publisher, phrases; publication year; etc., to satisfy various approaches of heterogeneous users. Automated cataloguing thus facilitates the searching by any search field in the OPAC. A number of standard library management both indigenous and international have such features in their cataloguing module. Notably, such features are used by many Indian libraries satisfactorily.

Authority file maintenance is another significant benefit of standard library management systems for automating cataloguing operations. These authority files are maintained by Authority control subsystem that supports the creation, maintenance and provision of access to different types of authority files such as vocabulary control file, name and title authority files, and tables of codes, etc. A good authority control subsystem is that which provides access to local or external authority files such as Library of Congress authority files from cataloguer's interface. Authority file is a tool used by cataloguers to create variant forms of names for authors, places, titles, subject headings, etc., used in bibliographic records. It provides controlled vocabulary and cross reference system for accessing bibliographic records. It enables librarians to provide uniform access to materials in library catalogues and to provide clear identification of author and subject headings. In automated cataloguing, the amount of time and effort expended in authority work can be reduced as external authority file entries can be imported and used to establish authority files in the system. Pertinently, some reputed Indian libraries are using this facility of cataloguing module. While in majority of libraries, the advantages of this facility remains to be seen.

The cataloguing module of all the library management packages helps in the preparation of shelf list and index files. The automatic preparation of shelf list helps in stock verification and proper arrangement of titles on stacks. While as preparation of index files help in searching of author index, subject index, keyword index, etc. Fortunately, many libraries in India are using these features available in the cataloguing module of their respective software packages.

It is also seen that the facility for generation of wide spectrum of statistical reports in cataloguing module of standard library management systems are other great utilities of automated cataloguing. Notably, the generation of these reports saves a substantial amount of professional time which could be utilized in providing other services to users. Appreciatingly, many Indian libraries generate almost all the reports related to cataloguing module. This availability of printed reports has reduced the user complaints about the illegible writings. Further, the generation of barcode and spine labels features is also available as in-built facilities in standard library software packages. It has been seen that many Indian libraries use these salient features, but manual spine labels have not been completely abandoned. However, there is a growing trend in large Indian libraries towards installing foreign library management packages wherein all such facilities are available within. In these libraries, it seems that these features will hopefully see the dawn of their utility very soon.

Regarding the usage of dictionary for entering data and select terms and thesaurus facility of standard library management packages, this feature is used in searching for synonyms as well as for broader and narrower terms to help in search and retrieval process. In the context of information storage and retrieval system, thesaurus reflects the specific needs, viewpoints and priorities of the users to be served by such a system. It aids the users in formulating their queries precisely and also acts as a tool to the indexer in assigning preferred description to the subject of documents. These facilities are used in almost all large Indian libraries, though Indian librarians' still need more training and time for the fuller understanding and usage of thesaurus and dictionary features.

The earlier Indian library software packages were not compatible for customization of reports either by the library staff while cataloguing or by the users at OPAC. However, the standard packages and newer versions are capable of this facility and consequently it is being used both by the library staff and users of Indian libraries to a considerable extent. The case is not much different in some international software packages which also were not compatible for these features earlier. However, since the development of modern and standard library management systems like that of Virtua, Alice for Windows, KOHA (open source software), etc., an enthusiasm is being seen among the users who are technically sound to customize their interests at OPAC. While among the librarians', a specialized person on directions from the concerned head is normally authorized to customize the reports in cataloguing module.

AUTOMATING CIRCULATION

Circulation control of libraries was probably one of the

first operation which got much attention worldwide. It is rightly said that the efficiency of any automated library system rests on the effectiveness of its circulation control. It is one of the technical operations of the library where user comes in direct contact with the library system. The users often were seen fed up of earlier manual circulation which was prolonged and time consuming as they had to waste much of their precious time in waiting at circulation counter for their interested resources. However with the automated circulation, these issues were solved as users are now issuing and returning their books themselves on self check-in and check-out stations. The automation of circulation section enhances the users' believability in the retrieval system of a particular library. The introduction of bar-coding system in libraries has shed the burden of manual circulation exercise to a large extent. Moreover, sending reminders through e-mail about the due date and fine imposed on late returns have also relieved the pressure of time consuming manual stamping of due date and error prone calculation of fines. Apart from eliminating the long queues at circulation counter, automated circulation is also very helpful in having greater control over loaned items. This pattern of opinion is uniform in all the libraries which have effectively automated its circulation section. The study carried out by (Oyemakinde and Evans, 1979) is also found inconsonance with this opinion. The manual circulation counter is shown diagrammatically below.

Fig. 20. Diagrammatical display of Manual Circulation Counter used in Traditional Libraries.

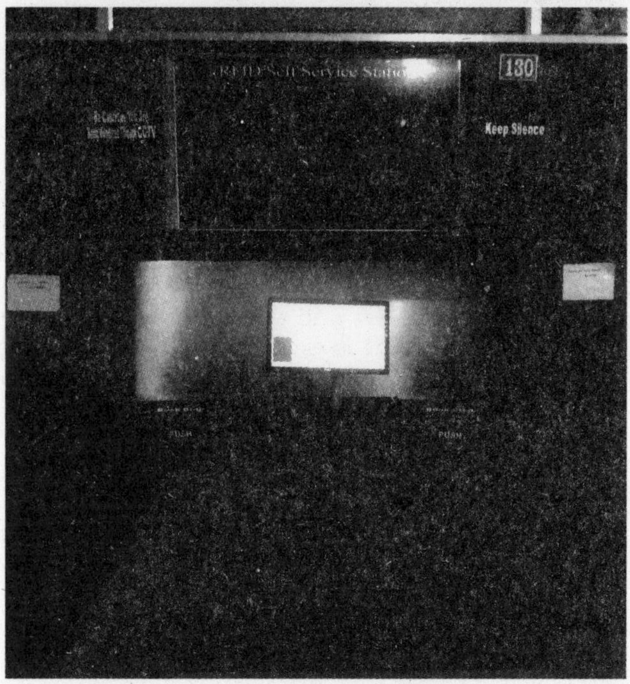

Fig. 21. Modern Automated User Oriented Circulation System (Self Check-in/Check-out)

Normally, any automated circulation system should possess following important features for its effectiveness and efficiency:

Table 4. Circulation Module

S.No.	*Features*
1	Creation of membership database of different categories with different parameters.
2	Generation of Patron ID card with required size of photograph and barcode number and blocking the membership as and when required.
3	Should facilitate easy manipulation of Patrons accounts, adding new patron account, reducing fine or updating patron information.
4	For lost, stolen and expiry cards, immediate generation of duplicate cards.
5	Shall possess bar code enabled services.
6	Supports integration with security system that compliments the self issue, self check-in/ check–out features.
7	Easy for staff to process loans, returns and circulation of library resources.
8	Facilitate Inter-Library Loan and makes it easy to keep record of both inward and outward loans.
9	Enable users to know the circulation statistics of resources and generates online queries of circulation statistics by both subject and membership category.
10	Supports tracking movement of requested items between branches to patrons and back to the central library system.
11	Allows users to reserve and staff to remove the reservation, if the reservation time is exceeded.
12	Allow the reservation for same resource more than once.
13	Supports automatic generation of due date slip and generates automatic reminders for overdue items.
14	Generation of fines for different kinds of resources automatically.
15	Supports grace period, if needed and fine exemption facilities for the poor members.
16	Provision to accept holidays while calculating fines.
17	Helpful in stock verification and printing of various types of statistical reports.
18	Facilitates to track the missing, lost, damaged, and weeded out materials.
19	Facilitates write off provision.
20	Circulation module shall support multi terminal systems, etc.

Circulation control has been one of the first applications of automated libraries during 1960s in the Western World (Haravu, 2004). There are various aspects of circulation transactions and consequently an automated circulation system is required to follow all the under mentioned functions:

- Check-out of materials
- Renewal of Loans
- Return of materials
- Identification of overdue materials
- Issuing of recalls for materials on loan
- Handling of fines
- Generation of reports and
- Preparation of offline notices (Reynolds, 1985)

In this background, one of the first online circulation systems had been installed in Illinois State Library in 1966. Another early online circulation system was implemented in late 1967 at Midwestern University in Texas (Reynolds, 1985). It has been rightly described by Atkinson that the circulation system should be one which would speak to the problems of its users rather than simply the problems of the library (Atkinson, 1972). After mentioning the background information of circulation system, the features and functions stated above will be described in the following paragraphs.

Most of the large Indian academic and research libraries are using most of the features of circulation module of their respective softwares. In the beginning of the session, the particulars related to new members are collected. Subsequently, this information is fed into the computer for further use. It is important to note here that all the libraries are collecting photographs also for putting scanned images along with the required information of the bonafide member. Almost all standard library management packages offer easy manipulation of users account and fine reduction. However, for existing members promoted to the next year of their study programs, only the updating of the information is required. In addition to this, the creation of the staff database is also possible. Needless to state, that the periodical updation is not required in membership file of the non-teaching staff or faculty of any institution or organization. The automated circulation is able to generate various membership files like that of faculty, staff, scholars and students with different kind of parameters set for different kinds of memberships. Such facilities are being used by many Indian libraries for issuing the resources to users according to their membership category. It is not surprising to mention here that there is a set parameter in almost all the Indian libraries to issue more books to the faculty as compared to other category of memberships. In case of faulty and mischievous users, the software can also block such membership with partial permissibility of return only or complete blocking of membership.

The automation of circulation section has undoubtedly brought a high degree of efficiency and accuracy in circulation control of libraries. The manual method was prone to several errors such as tremendous amount of difficulties in filing and making arrangement of hundreds of borrower cards as well as book cards. Now with the implementation of automated circulation, staff is feeling relaxed and accurate in filing entries. Furthermore, there is an increased usage of library collection due to automated environment. Though it is difficult to estimate the exact percentage of increased usage of library collection, however, the increased usage may range between 25-30 percent in comparison to manual operations. This factor may owe to the fact that the time taken in charging and discharging of an item in an automated circulation system is pretty less in comparison to the manual circulation. The borrower reluctant to visit the library having lesser amount of time are now often seen going and issuing the books while having their vacant time in the time table. As a matter of fact, it was often seen that due to the time consuming manual procedure, some students were quite reluctant in borrowing the documents from the libraries. Disappointingly, these students used to get bored while observing the long queues at the circulation counter.

The automation of circulation by any standard library management package like that of LibSys, Virtua, Alice for Windows, etc., has the ability to immediately generate the lost, damaged and stolen membership cards. But for this purpose, different libraries have different predefined parameters set for the generation of duplicate cards. In this background, some libraries take less time in providing duplicate cards, but not before certain formalities to be completed from users' end. While some libraries outsource the membership card production, hence users in such a kind of libraries are required to wait a bit longer in getting the duplicate borrower cards.

To ease the rush and long queues often seen at circulation counter during the manual transaction of books, the onset of bar code scanners have been very beneficial tool for speedy circulation of books in a large library set-up. Notably, these bar code scanners in a flash of second decode the string of white and black bar spaced codes of varying breadths fixed on the library books. The automated circulation system support bar code enabled issue and return services. Pertinently, such a facility is available in most of the large Indian libraries which issue and return with the help of bar code enabled devices. Though some few libraries are fully RFID enabled, however, bar code operations which come handy are being retained, because of electricity failure and inefficiency of some users with the RFID technology.

Another remarkable achievement out of the latest library technology has been self check-out and check-in facility to users. Needless to point out here that the use of this technology is popular in the libraries of Western World; nevertheless, a very few automated libraries of India has installed this technology as on date. A wonderful assertion is that some libraries, even though at far off remote places and with less infrastructural facilities as compared to that of some leading Indian libraries are providing self check-out/in facility to their users. On contrary, the IITs including some which are considered as champions of Indian library automation are still behind to provide RFID solutions in their libraries. In this connection, one research study also indicates that the user community prefers using self service process, because they can control the services better.

Although, the newer versions of Indian packages like that of LibSys software supports self check-out facility, but this facility is being used by only few libraries. While in some libraries scanner machines and other infrastructural facilities for self issue and return have been put in place. It is hoped that these libraries will sooner make such facilities operational. However, it is not surprising to point out here that most of the Indian libraries are yet to realize the benefits of self check-out and check-in facility. It may also be pointed out that these facilities result in minimum staff intervention in issue and return of books, besides that self check-out has further increased the usage of library resources and also generate an enthusiasm among user community particularly among the students. Consequently, the entire automated circulation scenario provides an opportunity for the librarians' to deploy the circulation counter staff for other productive services including reference service etc. It is also seen that the libraries which implement RFID technology and provide self check–in and check-out facilities effectively garner more footfall and readership than those which are still away from this wonderful and latest library technology.

Apart from these benefits of circulation system, automated circulation also helps in the analysis of the circulated items. This feature further helps in examining the acquisition related policies of the libraries. For instance, if a book is continuously issued or being put as a reserved item, the staff of these libraries advise the in-charge of acquisition section to start the process of procuring more copies of the same item.

Inter library loan facility is another attractive feature of automated circulation system, though it existed before in the name of library cooperation. Notably, it makes easy for staff to keep record of both inward and outward loans of accessioned resources to and from other libraries. It helps to access the resources of other libraries, if there is a formal agreement of resource sharing among two or more networked libraries. However, it is disappointing to mention here that only few libraries in India are using Inter-library loan facility, though available in their circulation module. The reason as stated earlier is the lack of formal agreement to share the resources with other libraries. It cannot also be ruled out that Indian librarians need a thorough training on this aspect. But, it needs to be mentioned here that many Indian libraries are the members of DELNET for this facility, while as IIT libraries share some resources with other established IITs in India. It is suggested that IIT libraries in India shall frame a formal agreement among them and other technical institutes of the country for sharing their resources via inter-library-loan sub-module. Similarly, central universities in India shall also undergo such an agreement for this purpose to ease the burden of collection development.

The provision of checking circulation and patron account statistics has been another boon of automated circulation as it has enhanced the users' library relations and reliability. Importantly users can take print out of the patron account and circulation statistics for clarification, if arisen, while calculating the fines on late return and remaining books on borrowers account. It has been seen that circulation module of standard library management packages help to check patron statistics. They provide comprehensive querying facilities based on both borrowers and subjects. It generates circulation statistics by both subject and membership category, whenever the need arises. The circulation statistics helps to know the highly circulated titles, most reserved titles and the users who use and borrow these titles. This helps in developing dynamic collection by ordering additional copies of most used titles if there are only few copies available in the library. Fittingly some libraries are using this facility, while the majority are yet to realize its benefits. In order to enhance the usage of library and its resources, some libraries have even initiated awards in this direction for most frequent users with highest transaction of library books.

Though the facility of tracking missing items, lost items, damaged items, weeded out items is available in the circulation module of leading library management packages, but majority of Indian libraries have not been using this facility. The main reason for it owes to the fact that departmental libraries of universities and other research organizations are not yet fully computerized. It is, therefore, difficult to track the circulation statistics of items that are available in these libraries. The software should also facilitate the provision of write off the lost, stolen, missing, damaged and not readable materials from the circulation records for its up-to-dateness.

Reservation and renewals in the academic and special libraries has been an important feature of any software as some books are often needed by a particular user community. In this direction, automated circulation of standard library software packages facilitates reservation and renewals. It is also possible for the librarians to remove the reservations in automated circulation, in case the time of reservation exceeds, though such feature may not be in practice in most of the Indian libraries. Therefore, there is a need to regulate the circulation of such items. This helps users to reserve the book of their interest in advance, if it is currently issued to some other user. The renewal feature of circulation module enables users to renew the loans of items that are already on their charge. There is, however, a predefined period of renewals and reservation set as per the policy of a particular library. In view of the importance of this feature, many libraries in India are using this facility.

Automated circulation is also capable to generate the fines according to different category of overdue resources leveled against different category of users. The automated circulation system, has however, posed a problem of fine and management of finances before the librarians. In manual system of circulation, librarians were free to wave-off the fines leveled for late return or sometime for lost resources, borrowed by users. They used to do it, in case of any request made by the poor students. Nevertheless, this privilege in an automated environment is lost as the system calculates the amount towards fine and concerned staff is left with very less options other than collecting the amount. Thus system ignores some times, the genuine requests of user community. However, some leading library software packages as mentioned earlier have the provision of waving-off the fines and facility of grace period. It seems that the librarians in India apparently need a thorough training for utilizing such important features of automated circulation control.

Moreover, the automation of circulation also helps in greater control over the issued items. In a manual circulation control section, sending the reminders and maintaining accurate due date was a tedious job. On contrary in an automated environment, libraries have been sending reminders through e-mail which is quite simple and easy, while as generation of due date slip is either not necessary or easy to generate.

Even if the circulation module of some leading library management packages used in Indian libraries have the provision to deduct the holidays while calculating the fines incurred upon overdue resources, however, only few libraries in India are using this facility as it exclusively exclude Sundays and other holidays of the calendar year while leveling the fines against the late return of books. With regard to other libraries, they do not use this feature; nevertheless, they level nominal overdue charges against late returns as compared to that of libraries in other countries.

It is worth mentioning here that during the training related to circulation module, librarians' shall show a great amount of interest in receiving the inputs with respect to the stock verification procedure. This training will help librarians in being quite optimistic with respect to stock verification process. The librarians are often under impression that the whole process of stock verification can be performed with the remarkable speed. The process of stock verification with the help of software may not have been conducted by many Indian libraries, though it is not that much difficult, if done through standard library management systems. Owing to the fact that RFID technology is yet to take place in majority of the Indian academic libraries, it remains to be seen that when automatic stock verification will be done in libraries. However, the other statistical reports feature generated automatically are used by many Indian libraries. The diagrammatic representation of automatic hand held inventory control device used for stock verification in modern libraries is shown below.

Fig. 22. Diagrammatic display of Hand Held Inventory used in Modern Libraries for Stock Verification.

In order to shed down the load of users on OPAC, the automated circulation is able to support many terminals that shall preferably be installed at the entrance of libraries. Needless, to mention that majority of the users are enthusiastically using OPAC as against card catalogue, though majority of Indian libraries maintain card catalogue also. Moreover the web-OPAC facility, available ..ow in many Indian and international library software packages shall be provided to users, who are overly loaded with projects and semesters and otherwise also running short of time to frequently visit the campus for using OPAC.

Nonetheless, the importance of more terminals has diminished with the advent of Web OPACs which besides campus of a particular institute serve beyond it, if kept on Wider Area Network (WAN). Thus, make users able to search their interests on OPAC at campus as well as at home.

AUTOMATING SERIALS CONTROL

Regarded as one of the most difficult library operations to automate, there would hardly be any Indian academic library which may have fully automated its serials control system. A full fledged automated serials control should normally possess following features which are discussed one by one hereafter:

Table 5. Serials Control Module

S.No.	*Features*
1	Enables easy input of serials data for check-in.
2	Enables easy selection/subscription of new journals initiated by the library and avoids duplication.
3	Helpful in efficient renewal and cancellation.
4	Enables easy accessioning of individual issue.
5	Keeps record of missing issues, damaged and faulty issues for subsequent replacement.
6	Supports the check-in of gap issues.
7	Enables to send automatic reminders for missing issues and claim for issues not received.

8	Helpful in preparation of list of holdings with their status.
9	Helps in maintenance of proper utilization of fund accounts for subscription and binding.
10	Maintains up-to-date binding file.
11	Supports printing of barcode labels for both bound and loose issues of serials.
12	Supports search and retrieval facility for staff within the module.
13	Enables Routing of periodicals.
14	Enables both simple and advance serials search facilities in web OPAC.
15	Enables to support union list of serials with other libraries.
16	Helps in easy invoice processing for both new subscription and renewal subscription.

Developing a module for serials control is the most difficult job for a developer and the operationalization of this module is equally tedious job for library staff. It will not be surprising to write that software vendors of almost all integrated library management systems receive the highest number of complaints from the clients regarding the serials control module. This majorly takes place because of several idiosyncrasies involved in the serials publications.

During early years of automation, the main application of computer with respect to serials control was the updating and printing of serials list (Reynolds, 1985). Historically, the concept of applying data processing techniques to serials began to attract attention as early as 1949 when punch-cards were used in serials procurement at the University of Texas Library (Steward, 1968). Later on, during 1960s, several libraries in US attempted to automate many procedures involved in serials control. One of the first to do so was the University of California.

It is being said that an automatic serials control module of any library automation software should perform the following functions:

- Ordering new journals
- Renewals of journals
- Discontinuation of journals
- Receiving the journals
- Sending the reminders
- Preparation of a list of received journals
- Keeping track of amount spent on the subscription of journals (Ravichandra Rao, 1983).

It is said that not many Indian automated libraries have started utilizing the serials control module of their respective software package. The primary reason for this delay as compared to automating other housekeeping operations may be that most of the academic libraries start the project with bound volumes of its serials collection initially. Once the library staff does not face any major problem in filing the entries of bound volumes, the other utilities of the serials control module are taken up accordingly. However, it is the most common experience of Indian librarians that they face number of issues in automating serials control and consequently require a high level of training on serials control module in order to get the fuller understanding of its versatile features for their effective usage. This opinion of requirement of high level training on serials module probably resembles with all Indian university and college librarians for fully operationalizing the serials control system of Indian libraries.

However, some libraries regarded as champions of Indian library automation like that of National Library, Kolkata; IIT Kanpur, INSDOC and IIT Delhi, etc., have been using serials control module right from the beginning of the automation process in their libraries, though barring some features. The automation of serials control helps by a way of easy inputting of serials data. The process saves a lot of time and also minimized the labor intensive sorting, filing and other paper handling routine work associated with the manual processing of serials. In this way, the library which automates its serials collection is also able to make the issues available to the users without much delay. The check-in subsystem of serials control module also helps in checking the duplication of issues which otherwise was a tedious and labor intensive process.

The functioning of serials control module is not fully seen in many large libraries in India. As a result of which, the details of each journal are entered and subsequently purchase order is generated. A check-in record is added to the bibliographic database and also the Kardex is updated with appropriate parameters. The inputting of details is done only once and the same information will be used everywhere in the serials control module. When any serials title is initiated, the system shows its status in the library. Thus, it eliminates the process of keying-in of data in case of already available serials titles.

The automation of serials control module is helpful in the process of renewal as well as cancellation of any periodical. In manual system, maintaining serials procedure was complicated and time taking in comparison to available utilities in an automated system. On contrary, automated serials control has made these procedures look easy and enabled easy accessioning of individual issues. However, accessioning of individual issue is not being done in most of Indian libraries. While as almost all automated libraries does accessioning of bound volumes. In case, any individual issue is found bigger in size, which is not quite common, then the library can go for accessioning individually.

Further, the serials control module also helps to maintain a record of missing issues. This facility helps in sending automatic reminders for the missing issues as well as gap issues. With this facility, libraries have been sending reminders through electronic mails. In a manual operation, the libraries use to send the reminders for missing issues through traditional mail system. Many times, it was experienced that these reminders did not reach to the destination. Sometimes, these reminders have reached to the destination with an unexpected delay. Moreover, it was costly method particularly when the reminders were sent abroad. On account of all these shortcomings, automated libraries have found the utility of sending automatic reminders and claim for not-received issues quite helpful in the serials module. However, majority of Indian libraries still use the manual method of reminders for such type of issues, though some leading softwares like LibSys, Virtua and Alice for Windows provides such versatile facility. It is beyond any doubt that Indian librarians, as has been said earlier also, require an exhaustive training in using these features of serials control module.

The Electronic Data Interchange (EDI) standards promote the system interoperability and appear as best hope for the claim process. But, unfortunately Indian libraries have not been found using this salient feature available in many Indian as well as foreign standard library packages. The notable to mention are LibSys, Alice for Windows and Virtua integrated library management systems.

The preparation of a list of holdings along with their status manually was quite time consuming and a tedious job. On the other hand, generating this list with the help of automated serials control system has been found very easy task and has saved an enormous amount of time of library staff. Wonderfully, many Indian libraries automatically generate the list of holdings of their serials collection.

The features regarding bindery is another wonderful facility of automated serials control. Earlier libraries were facing many problems in maintaining binding files, but with this facility available in the serials control module, their problems have been addressed by the newer and upgraded version of LibSys, Virtua and other standard library management softwares. It may also be outlined here that majority of libraries still maintain a manual binding file, though the facility of maintaining up-to-date binding file is more powerful in automated serials control. It seems that Indian librarians are yet lagging behind in using the robust features of automated serials control systems provided by leading software packages.

As mentioned elsewhere in the chapter, the generation of barcode labels can be done with the in-built facility in LibSys, Virtua, Alice for Windows and many other library software packages. Consequently, many libraries are using this feature of printing of barcode labels for both bound and loose issues of serials. While as in other libraries, the generation of barcode labels is still non-operational, though provision is available in many softwares. Some libraries are still using manual method of pasting labels on the journal collection of the library as the librarians find customization in some softwares a bit difficult, because of their technical inefficiency.

Like OPAC, the search and retrieval facility available in the automated serials module has been a wonderful benefit both for the staff and for the end users. Notably, this facility is functional in many Indian libraries and has been found saving a lot of precious time of the staff of these libraries. This facility lets both staff and users to search and retrieve their interests as per their requirement, more so users and staff are also able to customize their search and retrieval. The serials module of LibSys, Alice for Windows and Virtua softwares in particular facilitates simple and advance search facilities. It is, nevertheless, discouraging to note that the OPAC of many libraries is available only within their campuses over intranet and, therefore, the users of these libraries are able to use simple and advance search facilities only within the campuses. This may be because of the reason that these libraries might have some issues regarding web-OPAC facility with their vendors which hopefully will be sorted out soon and as a result they will shortly facilitate their users with this important facility. However in some libraries, users from across the country and abroad are able to access their serials collection over web-OPAC available on internet. Notably, this facility in libraries is largely being hailed by academic and intelligentsia community of the country. It has also saved precious time of faculty and scholars in particular; who need not to visit library/campus, in case their interested resources are unavailable in the library, as they can check their availability from anywhere, home, café, hotel, etc.

Although routing of periodicals facility is available in many Indian and international softwares such as LibSys, SOUL 2.0, Alice for Windows and Virtua, etc., but a handful of libraries in India may be using this feature of these integrated library systems. Notably, this facility helps to eradicate the biasness and favoritism often done in the manual routing of periodicals, as the system automatically generates the ID/name of the next user, to whom periodical as per rotation has to be issued. However for this purpose, user profile and periodical profile has to be maintained and matched up-to-date in the system, according to the interests of users. Moreover, the automated routing of periodicals enable frequent and equal usage of a particular periodical/article, which is in demand, without any discrimination to any user. But, it remains to be seen when this facility of serials control module will fully kick start in the Indian libraries.

In addition to above, the automated serials control also helps in easy invoice processing for the new subscription and also in case of renewal of periodicals, as it has largely reduced the manual and paper work which was error prone, besides difficult to maintain. It needs to be mentioned here that invoice processing for both new subscription and renewal is being carried out manually in majority of Indian libraries as the libraries majorly maintain a manual system of invoice processing. However, in view of growing interest of librarians towards automating serials control fully, invoice processing and other like features will be taken over by the automated system shortly, once the filing of entries is completed and detailed training is received by the vendor for full operationalization of the serials control module.

Another challenge for Indian librarians has been the compilation of Union catalogue. There are few rare agencies/research and development centers including NISCAIR and DRDO which take lead in compiling serials Union catalogue. One of such catalogues complied in India is National Union Catalogue of Scientific Serials in India (NUCSSI). Wonderfully many Indian as well as foreign library management packages possess the Union catalogue feature; however, disappointingly hardly any library in India is using this versatile feature available in integrated library systems. Though IIT libraries have been doing well in respect to Union catalogue, nonetheless, there has to be a formal agreement for compiling Union catalogue which is yet to be established in most of the libraries. In case of academic universities, their libraries are the members of DELNET and hence request it for the resources, if not available with them. Thus the story of Union catalogue among Indian academic libraries in particular is yet to be heard.

During the course of this research effort, it was also found that Indian libraries often face problems in the operation of serials control module. Librarians are often seen complaining to their vendors about their problems and request for solutions. Unfortunately, the vendors fail to provide solutions to most of the problems or solutions are provided after many requests and time gap. When this investigator contacted the representatives of LibSys (popularly used Indian integrated library package) for the sake of vendor performance, the vendor visiting for troubleshooting purposes, nevertheless, assured that they are about to provide a total solution in the next version of LibSys software. On other hand, Virtua people also reported that they are trying best to effectively manage the software across the country irrespective of the distance, though they too agreed with the author's realization with regard to difficulties in reaching to far off places.

Due to the proliferation of periodical literature in present era, automated serials control system plays a key role in managing this explosion. Though some libraries with special reference to IITs have been using serials control module of their package such as LibSys to some extent, but largely because of the lack of exposure, many academic libraries in India have till date nominally used this module, even if their library packages facilitates it. It is, therefore, recommended that the vendors should place more emphasis on imparting serials control training to librarians, who in-turn also need to be more enthusiastic in using all the relevant features available in the serials module.

This nominal use of serials control module is majorly seen in the accessioning of bound volumes in academic libraries. While as special libraries as mentioned earlier also use this module for many features like ordering, claiming, receipt and payments, etc. They also generate any desired report associated with periodical section. However, it may not be untrue to reveal that though these features have greatly lessened the burden involved in the manual acquisition of serials, nevertheless, the module is yet to provide the solution to all the problems of automating the serials system. These points also validate the study of (Cotta, 1989) wherein he also revealed the shortcomings found in an existing automated serials control system.

AUTOMATING ARTICLE INDEXING

Article indexing was once considered as the core of libraries serials collection as it provided the researchers with the abstract of newly arrived resources. However, with the availability of full text articles on internet at cheaper rates, this module has lost relevance in today's web world where millions of articles can be searched and retrieved at a faster and easier way.

An Indigenous software LibSys has another advantageous feature in the name of article indexing module which had great significance before the advent of full text articles. But for this, the librarians had to deeply involve their academic, intellectual and writing skills to draft the abstract/index of the periodicals/articles according to the interests of their users. In this regard, it has been observed that the article indexing module has lost its beauty in the present day libraries. Contemporary librarians are of the view that article indexing has lost the relevance in present era, where millions of full-text articles can be accessed via internet with more accurate results, because of least human error made during abstracting/indexing of articles. It is worthy to point out here that many Indian university libraries are subscribing a large number of international full-text online databases for free access to their users. It may also not be ruled out that the library staff is reluctant to go for the additional work in the periodical section. In another international software viz Virtua (increasingly used by Indian libraries), there is a separate module designed as a subsystem of serials control module of Virtua library management software to look after article indexing. However like LibSys software, the serials subsystem of Virtua is also used very rarely by Indian libraries owing to similar reasons.

RFID TECHNOLOGY IN LIBRARIES

Libraries have always been at forefront in implementing emerging information technologies to enhance the quality delivery of information services to their users (Kajewski, 2006). One such emerging information technology is RFID (Radio Frequency Identification) technology that has been attracting much attention since some years now. Technically, RFID is a blend of radio frequency based technology and microchip technology where-under information is contained on a microchip in form of tags which are fixed to books and is read by using radio frequency technology regardless of book orientation or arrangement (it does not require line of sight or a fixed place to read tags as traditional theft detection systems do) and the distance from an item is not a critical feature except in case of extra wide gates (Booktec Information, 2007). Some scholars also consider RFID as smart shelves and smart dump-bins that are technically feasible. Simply RFID is an identification technology that does the same job as barcodes do, but provide potentially a lot more benefits (Lindquist, 2003).

RFID is not a new technique or technology, but it has been the focus of British and Scottish scholars since World War II when they studied radio transmission system for IFF (Identification Friend or Foe) system to differentiate friendly aircraft from German planes (Melanie, Rieback and Andrew, 2006). In this system British, Germans, Japanese and American planes were installed with an IFF system which broadcasted a signal back to inform the radar crew on the ground that this was an allied aircraft. RFID technology is based on the same concept (Roberti, 2005). This technology, however, remained no longer limited to supply chains or logistic applications in defence aircrafts and other industries. But, some of its applications like anti theft detection and book checking out are also for library use. Since RFID has been around for many years now, but it was only with the advent of RFID tags which are made of low cost integrated circuits that enabled to use this technology at large scale to track and trace the item. Notably, the tags have their types like active RFID tags which posses a battery and transmits signal once external source is successfully identified, passive RFID tags which require an external electromagnetic field to supply power and facilitate signal transmission and battery assisted passive RFID tags which also require external source to wake, but have higher forward link capability providing greater range. Off these types, passive RFID tags are most suitable for library self checkout system, since no battery is needed (Hui, et. al., 2013). However, it has been seen that libraries began to use RFID as a substitute to their electromagnetic and barcode systems since late 90s (Mulla and Chandrashekara, 2006).

In developing world including India, RFID technology in university libraries is yet in infancy stage. In modern knowledge and learning environment, these libraries have to look for creative solutions in order to be relevant to the needs of users. In this direction, RFID is rapidly becoming the backbone of quality delivery and management of information in large libraries (Elisha, 2013). Significantly, the use of RFID reduces the time required for circulation operations. The most remarkable time savings are attributable to the fact that information can be read from RFID tags much quicker than from barcodes and that several items in a stack can be read simultaneously (Margam, 2010). It can be stated that RFID is mainly intended for change from partially automated to fully automated library system. Besides, RFID also offers great potential for broadening access to library services and security in ways never perceived earlier (Martin, 2011). It is said that large the collection a library possess, the more worthwhile would be to install RFID for the efficiency and effectiveness of its services.

Nevertheless like computerization, RFID technology too begun quite late in Indian libraries as compared to that of American and European libraries. Infact, there are only a handful Indian libraries including National Law

Institute Library; National Library; National Social Science Documentation Centre (NASSDOC), Central Library, Jawaharlal University; Central Library, Allama Iqbal Library; Jammu University Library; A C Joshi Library, Panjab University; Dr. Tulsidas Library, Post Graduate Institute of Medical Education and Research (PGIMER), Chandigarh; Pandit Deendayal Petroleum University, Ahmadabad; Nirma University, Ahmadabad; Chandragupta Institute of management, Patna; IIM Shillong; Jawaharlal Nehru Centre for advanced scientific research, Bangalore, etc., that have implemented RFID technology. However, with the advent of indigenous and international RFID compatible library softwares, there is presently an increasing trend towards implementing RFID in Indian university libraries.

With the paradigm shift from library to user, it becomes imperative for libraries to implement RFID technology in order to fulfill the users' demands effectively and efficiently. In one of the survey of RFID technology (*Hilal & mehtab, 2016*) conducted in university libraries in India, it is found that majority of the users totaling to 80% are effectively using self check-in/check-out machines for issue and return while about 19% still rely on staff for circulation transactions. Interestingly, users are quite enthusiastic to use the self check-in/out machines. Further, the rate of transaction of library resources per hour has also increased greatly after RFID implementation. The survey also reveals that a full majority of users with 89% students, 97% research scholars and 96% faculty members are either strongly satisfied or satisfied with services provided through RFID technology. There has been a dramatic change in the circulation of library resources after the implementation of RFID technology. It is seen that users have been by and large benefitted by this technology. The survey also suggests that the circulation and utilization of library resources have increased manifold after RFID implementation. Users are much enthusiastic in using the self issue and return system than relying on staff as RFID implementation has enhanced the transaction rate of books per hour to a great extent. This is largely because of the fact that RFID has more powerful features than manual circulation counter. Furthermore, users need not to stand in queues at circulation counter as was the practice before RFID for issuing or returning the books, thus saving a lot of users' precious time. Remarkably, RFID has saved a lot of time and exercise of staff consumed in circulation activities. This saved time and effort is being utilized in enhancing other operations and services as described by the librarians. It may further be mentioned here that self check-in and self check-out machines for issue and return of library resources have been discussed in detail in chapter 5 of this book. The RFID self check-in and check-out machines for self issue and return of library books is also diagrammatically shown as under.

Fig. 23. Diagrammatic representation of the Self Check-in/ Check-out Station

Being a developing economy, high costs are always considered as major challenge of RFID technology; nevertheless, with decline in the costs of RFID equipments, there is an increasing trend towards RFID technology in Indian libraries. Undoubtedly there are some limitations; however, the definite benefits of RFID as mentioned above cannot be sidelined to fully automate the library services to meet the pressing demands of techno-oriented users in an effective way. It is also foresighted that there will be a mass adoption of RFID technology in near future, because of the change in policy by the State Governments and University Grants Commission for providing adequate funds for automating Indian college and university library system.

It is a general perception that a large number of India librarians feel that the manual operations had become mind-numbing and monotonous while automated environment has enhanced job satisfaction level due to diversity in these operations. Interestingly, the more number of librarians in IIT libraries are of this opinion as that of academic libraries. This view of IIT librarians owes to the fact that IITs organize periodical training programs on fundamentals of information technology. Significantly, they take more interest in attending these training programs. Notably, these training programs grow keen interest in the procurement of library automation software to work in an automated environment. However, Indian academic libraries and librarians lag behind in this respect, though some university libraries send their staff to different organizations and agencies for attending such training programs. The acquaintance of more technical knowledge among the library staff of IITs may be the reason that they are more efficient in handling and managing automated library systems than the staff of academic libraries.

Since the needs vary from a library to library, because of their heterogeneous users and collection, therefore, the selection of library management package should majorly be based on the requirements of a particular library. It is, however, always advisable that before the selection of a standard library package, the library staff shall necessarily undergo a thorough training on each module of the software for effective operationalization of all the relevant features.

The onus also lies on the librarians to periodically undergo for the training courses on automation conducted separately across the country by renowned organizations including NISCAIR, DRDO, DESIDOC, ISI, DRTC, etc. However, the courses like PGDLAN (Post Graduate Diploma in Library Automation and Networking) taught in many Indian universities can better serve the purpose of managing automated library system effectively and efficiently. Librarians shall also press upon the vendors for detailed periodical training programs on all the available modules both at onsite and offsite under the realistic terms and conditions, before the procurement of library management package.

It may also be pointed out here that a number of Indian academic and special libraries maintain an up-to-date OPAC which enables users in easy and fast searching of their interested resources within a click of a button on the computer terminal. Keeping in view the practical relevance of service side of OPAC, it has been, therefore, discussed in detail in the automated information services in the chapter to follow.

REFERENCES

Atkinson, H. C. (1972). *The Ohio System online circulation system: Proceedings of the 1972 Clinic on Library Applications of Data Processing.* Urbana: University of Illinois, p. 23.

Booktech, Information (2007). *LibBest library RFID Management System.* Retrieved December 25, 2013 from www.rfid.library.com/

Cotta, M. Von (1989). Automation and Academic Library Structure. *Libri,* 39(1), 47-63.

Elisha, O. M. (2013). Adoption of Radio Frequency Identification Technology in University Libraries: A Kenyan Perspective. *The Electronic Library,* 31(2), 208-216.

Haravu, L. J. (2004). *Library Automation Design, Principles and Practice.* New Delhi: Allied, pp. 69-150.

Harrison, K., & Summers, D. (1988). Development of an Automated Acquisition System at the University of Lancaster Library. *Program,* 22(2), 143-162.

Hilal, A., & Mehtab, A.A. (2016). *Library Automation in India : An Evaluative Study.* New Delhi : Ane Books, pp. 132-133.

Hirshon, A. (1988). Vision, Focus and Technology in Academic Research Libraries. In Joe A. Hewitt (Ed.)., *Advances in Library Automation and Networking* (Vol.2, pp. 215-257). Connecticut: JAI Press.

Hui, W., Luk, B.L., & Liu, L.K.P. (2013). EPC RFID Technology for Library Applications. *Measurement and Control.* 46(1), 26-30.

Kajewski, M.A. (2006). Emerging Technologies changing Public Library Service Delivery Models. *APLIS,* 19(4), 157-163.

Lindquist, M. G. (2003). RFID in Libraries_Introduction to the Issues. *Proceedings of World Library and Information Congress: 69th IFLA General Conference and Council, 1-9 August, 2003,* Berlin. Retrieved December 24, 2013 from www.ifla.org/w/ifla69/papers116lindquist.pdf.

Melanie, R. R., Bruno, C., & Andrew, S.T. (2006). The Evolution of RFID Security. *IEEE Pervasive Computing.* 5(1), 62-69

Margam, M. (2010). RFID Technology Implementation in Two Libraries in New Delhi. *program: electronic library and information systems,* 44(2), 149-157.

Martin, Z. (2011). Radio Frequency Identification (RFID): Time to take another Look. *OCLC's Systems and Services: International Digital Library Perspective,* 27(2), 146-154.

Mulla, K.R., & Chandrashekara, M. (2006). Application of RFID in Libraries for Physical Information Security – a View", *Proceedings of 4th International Convention CALIBER-2006, Gulbarga 2-4 Feb, 2006, INFLIBNET Centre,* Ahmedabad. Retrieved December 29, 2013 from http://ir.inflibnet.ac.in/bitstream/1944/1100/1/56.pdf.

Oyemankinde, A. (July, 1979). Automation at Ibadan University Library. *Program,* 3(3), 143-146.

Rajgopalan, G. (1981). Computerized Book Acquisition. *Journal of Library and Information Science*, 6(2), 84-91.

Ravichandra R., I. K. (1983). *Library Automation*; DRTC Refresher Seminar. Bangalore: DRTC, pp. 149-161.

Reynolds, D. (1985). *Library Automation Issues and Applications.* New York: R. R. Bowker, pp. 29-408.

Roberti, M. (2005). The History of RFID Technology. *RFID Journal.* Retrieved November 12, 2014 from http://www.rfidjournal.com/article/view/1338/1.

Steward, B. W. (1968). Automated Serials System in Perspective. In Stephen R. Salmon (ed.)., *Library Automation: A State of the Art Review* (p. 131). Washington, D.C: ALA.

Woods, R. G. (1986). Library Automation in British Universities. *Program,* 20(4), 359-381.

5

Automated Information Services

This chapter as suggested in the above title deals about the information services provided to the users in an automated environment. Further, the details about many functions and services wherein the end users come in direct contact with a particular automated library system have been discussed. The chapter also throws light on many automated search services including CAS, SDI, bibliographic services and electronic document delivery services. Furthermore, it describes in detail the users' point of view of OPAC. The services and functions have been correlated with some of the leading and popularly used standard library management packages by Indian college and university libraries.

BACKGROUND

In the preceding chapter, back-end automation or automation of housekeeping operations was discussed in detail. To kick start the automated information services, it is essential to know about the term. It is actually that essential part of the entire library automation project, where users of any particular library come in direct contact with the library and its retrieval system. It can be said that the entire efficiency of any library automation project rests on the satisfaction of users with that project. A good automation project can entirely go either way, if its users are not satisfied with it. In this context, it can be stated that user satisfaction constitutes the centre stage of automated information services. There are a number of factors which directly or indirectly influence the entire automation project which have been discussed here. Simply speaking, for the better and fuller understanding of the automated information services or front end automation of a good automation project, it should comprise many constituents/services. These constituents have been discussed and illustrated separately under different headings in following pages.

AUTOMATED LIBRARY SERVICES

The application of integrated library management softwares in different operations and services of libraries has brought their resources to the doorsteps of their users. Users can now access their desired resources sitting at home without physically visiting the library. Needless to mention that automated library system has brought otherwise underused/unused library resources to the notice of users, thereby had a great impact on their usage. The increased usage of library resources due to automated library systems in place perhaps represents the national consensus. However, there is some percentage of population of users, though less in number who does not agree with this opinion. This number of users may belong to that category which is either uncomfortable in using technological gadgets for library services or are technically less skilled to use automated library services.

Further, some users are also neutral in viewing the influence of automation of libraries on usage of its resources. These users may belong to that population of users who don't want to change their information seeking behavior with the modern and automatic trends taking place in modern and automated libraries around the world.

It is said that a high majority of users in Indian libraries are of the opinion that library automation/ softwares are tremendously benefitting them as they are now more tempted to visit the library and use the resources. On contrary they were reluctant to visit the library previously, because they used to face difficulties in consulting card catalogues. Often, users find that the filing of these cards is not up to the mark and difficult to update. Sometime, even cards are missing while books are found on shelves. Moreover, it is a tedious and laborious job. On the other hand, within a fraction of a minute, users are able to locate any resource of the library via OPAC even sitting at home.

Remote access facility is another wonderful facility of automated library system which has raised the usage of library resources to a great extent. Some libraries in India such as Kashmir University library provides this facility to the users sitting at any part of the world. The resources with special reference to electronic databases will greatly help users particularly researchers and faculty members for carrying out non-stop research and development work even beyond their campuses especially during the occasions of Sundays/holidays and after the closing hours of their institutions.

It can be said that automation has undoubtedly greatly enhanced the level of usage of library resources in all automated libraries in India. This opinion of increased usage of library resources is also substantiated with the findings of some earlier scholars like Kreslin O'Brein, and Smith (1994) and Sajjad ur Rehman and Reham (2010). The increased usage of library resources due to automation of various operations and services has also been reported by another foreign study conducted by (Peake, 1981). This study was also related to university libraries, though of a foreign country.

SEARCH SERVICES (OPAC AGAINST CARD CATALOGUE)

With the introduction of integrated library management systems, the means of searching and retrieving information has shifted from manual to online methods. Significantly, OPAC has been remarkable invention to enable users to search and locate their interested resources within a flash by clicking the desired button on the keyboard. In technological institutions of the country, majority of users are using OPAC against card catalogue for locating and identifying their desired resources in the library collection. This is because that their users are more techno savvy as of the users of academic universities and colleges in India. This situation in academic libraries is not encouraging where manual methods are yet operational, though in many libraries automation has been in full swing since the UGC and INFLIBNET efforts for automating college and university libraries in India have picked up the momentum.

It has been, however, seen in some libraries that OPAC has not completely replaced manual methods, as some users particularly in academic libraries still make use of card catalogue for searching purpose. While as a good number of Indian users use both OPAC and card catalogue for searching library resources. Since OPAC takes less time and provides many access points besides being user-friendly as that of card catalogue, Indian users towards using OPAC for searching library resources are growing at very fast rate. At the same time, the usage of card catalogue, because of its many issues like single point access, ineligible writing, shabby and torn cards is declining day after day. However, some card catalogue users are used to it, and are, therefore, carrying on using the card catalogue. In some cases, OPAC terminals are sometimes busy and users are waiting for their turn. In that case, users can find no crowd around the trays of card catalogue; hence, they can directly go to use these cards in trays. It may be mentioned here that this category of users may belong to those who cannot afford to wait.

Notwithstanding the fact that automation has replaced most of the manual operations, many large Indian libraries still maintain the manual catalogue cards, though used nominally. This kind of phenomenon is also witnessed in most libraries of the developing countries primarily due to the erratic power supply. Thus, a manual catalogue card comes as a rescue in these times of emergency. Besides this, sometimes there is a problem in library software and during the trouble-shooting, library doors cannot be closed. At this point of time, card catalogue comes as a rescue during these crises. Some Indian librarians also feel apprehensions with regard to data loss due to virus or other problems in soft version of the data; hence, they maintain the hard copy in the form of card catalogue. Some university libraries in India recently experienced hacking of their websites and other important data due to which the online library facilities had to be shut for some time. This phenomenon of OPAC is also highlighted by some other authors like Mehtab and Amita in 2008. The traditional card catalogue and modern OPAC have also been shown diagrammatically below.

Fig. 24. Diagrammatic display of Traditional Manual Catalogues in the Card Cabinet in Allama Iqbal Library, University of Kashmir, Srinagar

Fig. 25. Diagrammatic representation of Modern OPAC of Maulana Azad Library, Aligarh Muslim University, India

SEARCH STRATEGIES IN OPAC

The most powerful feature of any up-to-date OPAC is the availability of different search options. Generally speaking, there are two broad search approaches in almost all the library OPACs - the basic search and the advanced search. In basic search which is also called as simple search, users can first select a single search field like keyword and then enter the term that they wish to search for. The other kind of broad approach of search i.e. advanced search or sometimes called as guided search, enable users in combining of terms from one or more fields with the use of Boolean operators such as AND, OR, NOT, truncation, etc. It may be stated here that this kind of search option is primarily used to narrow or broaden the search.

As far as using the search strategies in OPAC is concerned the more the users are technically sound the more effectively will search strategies be carried out. In a country like India, where digital literacy is yet below than the developed countries, effective search strategies will remain to be seen. However in the libraries of technological institutions, majority of users are making good use of the available search strategies in their libraries' OPAC. In case of academic libraries, most of the users prefer simple search in OPAC, while as some advanced users also use advance search options available in the OPAC. The techno savvy users as has been said earlier use all kinds of search options in OPAC for locating their books/resources in the library.

It may also be stated here that many Indian users make use of both simple and advance search options in OPAC. As mentioned elsewhere in the chapter, some users are still uncomfortable in using OPAC and, hence, carry on using manual methods for search and retrieval purpose, though some of these users are also acquainted with computer skills.

As far as search strategy is concerned, this study like many other studies, also found that a high percentage of users in Indian libraries prefer simple search option in OPAC. This vast number of users may have never used advanced search, because what they intended for, they got through simple search.

It is interesting to note here that some users are formulating advance search strategy. Expectedly, this number of users, as against the users of academic libraries, is found more in the technological institutions as they are technologically competent in using such kind of searching in other application softwares. It may also be stated here that some users in Indian libraries are found using simple as well as complex searches.

SEARCH PRIORITY IN SIMPLE AND ADVANCED SEARCH MODE

Search priorities of users, while searching on OPAC, often vary from person to person depending largely on the technological competency of an individual user. More so as discussed earlier, the students of technological institutions anywhere in the world dominate different kinds of complex search options as against the students who belong to non-technological institutions. In Indian libraries, it is largely found that users use simple search wile locating the availability of their books on OPAC while as a small number of users use complex search facilities in OPAC.

There are generally different search options in the OPAC of automated libraries. These search options comprise author search, title search, subject search, publisher search and call number in simple search mode and phrase search, Boolean operators i.e. And, OR and Not, truncated search etc., in advance search mode. In academic libraries of India, most of the users use title and author search in simple search facility since they are easy to remember than call number and publishers' name. These search options almost satisfy the major requirements of users. The author search facility lets the users to search the book by a specific name of the author to restrict their search term to author database only, thereby saves the time of users. However, the title search is probably more common particularly among academic libraries. It lets users to retrieve their requested sources from title database leaving all other approaches aside. Thereby, it increases the user satisfaction by enhancing precision and recall of the results. It may also be stated that the subject search facility is intended for those users, who do not know or remember the exact author or title of the document they aim for. Instead, such types of users browse their interested sources by subject search. Thus, it enhances the user satisfaction

In case of special libraries attached with research and development institutes, they also use advance search facilities as stated above. Besides, they are also in position to use search options like journal title, ISBN, ISSN, etc. However, it is observed that these search options are rarely used by the users.

Some users also prefer Boolean search to limit their search option and save their time. The Boolean search comprise AND, OR and NOT operators which are used to combine the terms with any of the combinations available in advanced search mode in OPAC. The usage of Boolean operators also directly depends upon the technical capability of users. Among the three Boolean operators, 'AND' operator is being used more, while the other two operators namely 'OR' and 'NOT' are comparatively used lesser. Notably, the use of these Boolean operators helps users to broaden or limit their search term which in turn increases the precision and recall of the search results.

Wonderfully some users, though in small number, also use other complex search options available in advanced search mode in the OPAC of Indian libraries. There is another advance search option such as phrase search which is also used by some users, though very nominally. It may be noted here that phrase search facility lets the users to search the exact document titles such as journal title, book title, etc. Besides this, it also helps to find the specific search string in different sources.

Another complex search option available in OPAC is 'truncation'. Pertinently truncation is a search facility, whereby a search can be conducted for all different forms of words having the same common root. Thus, it saves the time of users by merely inputting some suffix letters of a truncated word i.e. truncated word comput* will retrieve items like computer, computing, computation, compute, etc. This kind of truncation is called as right truncation. The case is somewhat similar with regard to prefix truncation i.e. truncated word '*hyl' will consequently retrieve items on methyl, ethyl, etc. This type of truncation is called as left truncation. This search facility is also used very rarely in Indian libraries mainly because of its technical requirement which most of the users in academic libraries are short off.

Besides the above discussed facilities, a good OPAC also provide some other advanced search options such as:

Proximity Search

This search facility lets the users to specify whether the two search terms should occur adjoining to one another Or whether one or more words occur amid the search terms Or whether search terms should occur in the same paragraph irrespective of intervening words, and so on. The operators used for this search facility varies from one search system to another.

Field Specific Search

This is that search facility which can be conducted either on all fields in database or may be restricted to one or few chosen fields for high precision. Specific fields and codes differ in accordance to search system and database.

Limiting Search

Here user may limit a given search by using his desired criteria like language, year of publication, type of source, etc.

Range Search

This type of advance search facility is very useful with numerical and statistical information. This type of search facility is mainly useful in selecting records with certain data ranges. However, all these search options are used rarely, because of their complexity in nature. Nevertheless, some users particularly among the IITs, IIMs and other technical institutions are seen using these complex search options in advanced search mode of OPAC.

A skillful help desk will greatly be helpful for new entrants with special mention of freshers and Arts background students in academic institutions, to guide them in using the OPAC and its advance search techniques for the effective utilization of library resources.

OPAC FOR STATUS OF MATERIALS

The main objective of any library user using its OPAC is to know the availability of his/her desired resource/book in the library collection. Since a large number of Indian university libraries, IIT libraries and other libraries attached with research and development organizations maintain an up-to-date OPAC, therefore, a majority of users use OPAC for checking the status of resources as desired by them. However, there is still a considerable population of users in Indian academic libraries who are yet away from the benefits of such a wonderful facility of automated library system. This situation in far off colleges and universities is even more dismal where the automation of libraries is yet a distant reality. However, it cannot be denied that some potential and prospective users find more pleasure and comfort in minutely searching the shelves of the library for their desired interests manually, though the manual method is unanimously regarded as time consuming and laborious. Nonetheless, it has its own charm of finding alternative interests/ books, in case the actual desired book is not found. This category of users also do not shy in taking help of library staff, whenever they felt.

A wonderful observation is that a large number of users check the status of books via OPAC. Meaning thereby, this user community does not go to seek the help from library staff regarding the availability of any book, rather, they search their desired resources on their own in the OPAC. Expectedly, this number of users is more in case of technological institutions as that of academic universities and colleges. This may again be because of the fact that these users are more techno savvy than the users' of academic libraries.

OPAC FOR LOANED MATERIALS

Another worth noting advantage of a well maintained OPAC is that it also provides the facility of knowing, who has borrowed what? and what is the due date of a loaned resource. This facility lets the users of a particular library to know the status of their desired resources. Users can also know the due date of a particular book, if currently on loan to someone else through this facility. It is widely regarded that this facility available in the OPAC is used by large number of Indian users, though a considerable percentage of users are still away from taking benefit of it. This viewpoint is also found in academic libraries where many users use this facility of checking the status of loaned items on OPAC. However, the users of academic libraries cannot compete with the users of technology oriented institutional libraries in using this facility as they are quite familiar in using the advance search techniques.

The onus here lies on the librarians particularly academic librarians to conduct some orientation or if need arises a detailed training program by a skilled professional for the new users for using such kind of important facilities in the OPAC effectively. These programs can be arranged in a roster wise with predefined number of students and subjects/ departments on each day, so as to cover the program rapidly. This will acquaint all the users about the different technicalities in using the library resources without wasting any time. Such training programs shall be the part of admission policy or extra curriculum in the colleges and universities of India. It is no wonder to point out here that a fairly good number of users in Indian libraries are still away from using this important facility, though their libraries maintain this facility up-to-date. It apparently shows the ignorance of Indian library users towards using automated libraries effectively and efficiently.

SELF CHECK-OUT/ CHECK-IN

The self check-out /check-in feature of any integrated library management system simply relieves the library staff of a particular library from the laborious and time consuming circulation activities of books. Needless to mention that it saves a lot of time of users as they need not to wait in long queues which is a common feature often seen at the circulation desk for issue and return of books in any library, where self check-in/out system is not in place. As a result, it enhances the user satisfaction on circulation control system of a library.

As mentioned elsewhere in the book, the self check-out and check-in system in the majority of Indian libraries is yet to take place fully, though some measures have been taken by some leading university libraries and special libraries of India. But, it largely remains to be seen when all the large libraries will kick start this wonderful facility, though other operations and services are automated. On contrary, the facility for self check-out/check-in through 3M machine in some university libraries such as Jawaharlal Nehru University Library, Mysore University Library, Kashmir University library and some more libraries is in full swing. Remarkably, a large number of users in these institutions are seen issuing and returning the books and other library resources themselves via self check-out/in stations operational at different prominent positions.

There is a great enthusiasm and rush among the user community for using self check-out/check-in system in these libraries. Moreover, an indigenous survey (*Hilal & Mehtab, 2016*) shows that the student category is using this facility more followed by research scholars and faculty members. This facility of self issue and return has raised the image of libraries retrieval system among the vast user community. Pertinently, all sections of users in these university libraries have hailed this initiative of librarians and other information professionals involved in making this facility a reality in Indian libraries.

INTERFACE OF OPAC

Seen from the users' point of view, the user-friendliness of OPAC is most important aspect of any automated library system. It is beyond any doubt that user-friendly interface of OPAC always enhance the overall utilization of library resources and its other services, as it majorly saves precious time of users. In this background, it is seen that the majority of the standard library management packages provide user friendly interface of OPAC with some exceptions. The interface of SOUL software is for example user friendly than other Indian library management packages, but it has its own limitations in providing other services. The LibSys software on the other hand has been found more user friendly with all other operations and facilities equally capable of supporting the international standards. In case of foreign library software packages, though Virtua has been fulfilling all the international standards and is more robust in its features and functions than any other software package. But, its user friendliness has been questioned by a number of Indian libraries and their users. In this connection, one of the studies of LibSys and Virtua library management packages conducted among IIT Delhi, IIT Kanpur and Kashmir University by Hilal and Mehtab in 2016 reveal that 54.54% students, 67.85% research scholars and 70.37% faculty members in IIT Delhi strongly agree that the interface of OPAC of LibSys software is user-friendly. A slight difference has been witnessed in IIT Kanpur, where 59.23% students, 66.66% research scholars and 68% faculty members strongly agree in this regard. In comparison, a reasonably low number of users in Kashmir University with 22.59% students, 27.5% research scholars and 34.61% faculty members view the interface of their OPAC user friendly. Their study further shows that a considerable percentage of users with 30.90% students, 22.61% research scholars and 25.92% faculty members in IIT Delhi place their opinion about the user friendliness of OPAC in not so friendly category. This situation is almost parallel in IIT Kanpur; where 26.63% students, 20.83% research scholars and 28% faculty members also possess same opinion about OPAC. However in Kashmir University, more number of users with 27.64% students, 35% research scholars and 30.76% faculty members perceive that the interface of Virtua OPAC is not so friendly to use.

Though the majority of users in IIT Delhi, IIT Kanpur and Kashmir University found their OPAC user friendly, but a considerable percentage in Kashmir University reported that the Virtua OPAC is not as friendly as its earlier used SOUL software. The case is somewhat different in IIT Delhi and IIT Kanpur where a small percentage of users opined that the LibSys OPAC is not friendly. This number in Kashmir University as against the IIT Delhi and IIT Kanpur is a matter of concern for its library administration. The scholars, however, reveal that this may largely be because of the inadequate skills of users to use Virtua OPAC effectively. Further, this number may belong to the users who still rely on manual methods as discussed earlier. In case of IITs, some users also rely on manual methods, because of being uncomfortable with automated library system. This category may belong to the subjects like social sciences and humanities where information technology has, but not so wider application as compared to other subjects.

Based on the above facts, it is advisable for Indian librarians that the interface and user friendliness of OPAC shall be one of the prior considerations while attending the demonstration of a particular package by the vendors, as user friendly OPAC leads to user satisfaction of the library.

THE INFORMATION RETRIEVAL

The proliferation of literature in diverse fields posed great challenges before information manages for fast and accurate information access to users. Thus librarians had to automate their retrieval system as per the demand of the day to serve the users effectively. In any automated library system, information retrieval system constitutes the vital subsystem of entire library automation project. It may not be wrong to state that retrieval system of a particular library is directly proportional to its users' satisfaction. Rather, it is more appropriate to mention that the success of whole automated library system rests on the effectiveness and efficiency of its information retrieval system. Information retrieval is actually a process of selecting information from some repertoire i.e. usually from libraries. It chiefly helps a user who desires to get some information which could be related to his research, decision making and other related fields, etc. Automated information retrieval services constitute three basic components- the database (eg. MEDLINE, INSPEC, COMPENDEX, BIOSIS, etc.), the user and the blend of technology (i.e. tools, techniques, gadgets, etc.) which bridge the digital divide between user and the database. The automated information retrieval system is also called as intelligent retrieval system. Presently, there are many library software packages in India and abroad which help libraries in maintaining up-to-date information retrieval services for the benefit of their users. These software packages notably comprise LibSys, Tulips, Virtua, Alice for Windows, MINISIS, etc., as discussed in chapter-3. The beauty of information retrieval system is that it can retrieve both exactly matched query and partially matched query. In this system, a number of search techniques such as proximity search, range search, limit search or other advance searches are used.

It is seen that some large Indian university libraries maintain an up-to-date information retrieval system. However, the retrieval system of many libraries is not worth noting. In this light, the researcher tried to assess the retrieval system of some Indian libraries by setting different parameters in one of the surveys'. In view of these parameters, it has been observed that 14.54% students, 19.04% research scholars and 14.81% faculty members in IIT Delhi rate the retrieval system of LibSys library management package as excellent. Not much difference has been observed in IIT Kanpur, where 13.58% students, 18.05% research scholars and 8% faculty members also rated the retrieval system of LibSys software as excellent. Surprisingly the retrieval system of Kashmir University Library has been found better than these IITs. Notably, 26.68% students, 35% research scholars and 26.92% faculty members have displayed their opinion in excellent category. The difference observed therein may be because of the reason that Kashmir University library is effectively providing self check-in/ check-out facility while as such facility is yet to be fully operational in most of the Indian libraries including IIT Delhi and IIT Kanpur. Similarly, more users in Kashmir University library have rated the retrieval system of Virtua software package used by the library between very good and good parameters. The corresponding figures in other libraries are found lesser as that of Kashmir University library.

Shockingly, 16.72% users in IIT Kanpur and 14.05% in IIT Delhi have rated the retrieval system of LibSys software used by their libraries in average and poor category. This number has been found less in Kashmir University as only 8.49% users have rated this viewpoint. While as disappointingly some users with 3.33% students and 1.19% research scholars in IIT Delhi and 3.80% students and 2.77% research scholars in IIT Kanpur find their library's retrieval system as poor. Like other parameters, this parameter too has got thinner response in Kashmir University, where a meager 1.92% students have placed the retrieval system in poor category.

The findings clearly suggest that the retrieval system of those Indian libraries which provide self check-in and self check-out facilities are appropriately rated ahead as that of non self check-in and check-out system libraries. It is also seen that the users are more enthusiastic in using self check-out/in stations. As pointed out earlier in the chapter, this facility is yet to take place fully in most of the Indian libraries including that of IITs which are regarded as institutes of national importance.

RFID technology with self check-out/in facility and biometric stock verification is the most modern technological application used to ease the pressure on circulation and efficient inventory control. It is suggested that like those libraries which have implemented this technology, other Indian academic and special libraries should also make use of such modern technology to enhance their retrieval system.

AUTOMATED CURRENT AWARENESS SERVICE (CAS)

For any scholar, of whatever capacity, it becomes necessary for him/her to keep himself/herself active and vibrant in his her desired field. He/she would also be required to know the other developments which influence and impinge his/her field. This approach of information is called as current approach and any service which is intended to satisfy this current approach is called as current awareness. As the title suggests, it shall be very fast and up-to-date. But like other services, this service also had taken a hit in manual libraries. However, with the advent of computers in libraries and their application in aiding current awareness service, it became fast and vibrant. The automation of libraries made these services economical, easy and very simple. The most vital aspect of current awareness service is the speed with which this service is provided to the users.

According to Kemp (1979), Current awareness services broadly constitute two types viz in-house or locally generated current awareness service and current awareness services provided by external databases. Kemp further discusses these as under:

In-House/Locally Generated CAS

At the initial stage of automation in Indian libraries, skillful Indian librarians and information professionals were generating manual bibliographic database by scanning journals, newspapers, magazines, patents and other sources. These scanned images were then put on the LAN of the institute or the library and were sent to their desired users in electronic form from the in-house database. However, with the inception of standard integrated library management systems in Indian libraries, the pattern of in-house generated current awareness services was replaced by current awareness service by external databases, though in-house databases are still holding validity in some Indian libraries. Some of the softwares which were popular in generating in-house current awareness service are BASIS, BRS/SEARCH, CAIRS, ORBIT, etc.

CAS by External Databases

Current awareness service by external databases means that the service is subscribed by the library which after subscription is provided to users on user name and login passwords. There are majorly two types, the online hosts and the database producers.

- In online hosts, the services provided are chiefly generated from the database mounted by these hosts. The online hosts also provide save search facility which stores profiles that can be run on daily basis.
- In database producers' current awareness service, there are plethora of publishers and database producers across the globe offering current awareness service on different subjects. Libraries have the liberty to select the desired database producers and the CAS provided by them. Some examples in this regard are:
- ISI alerting service,
- Table of contents alerting service,
- American Chemical Society (ACS) alert service,
- Elsevier science,
- Sage publications,
- Institute of Physics,
- Dialog alert service, etc. (Kemp, 1979).

All these types are provided to users in an automated environment by means of displaying them in the pattern of flash news on library's web page. Indian libraries though sometimes make a telephone call also to users about the latest arrivals and other alerting services. Such services are, however, available in special and research libraries than academic libraries.

SELECTIVE DISSEMINATION OF INFORMATION SERVICE (SDI)

This is an information service of an organization which concerns itself with machine assisted channeling of new items of information from whatever sources to those points within the organizations where the probability of usefulness in connection with the current work or interest is high (Luhn, 1961). Selective dissemination of information according to Richards (1992) mainly comprises following four components:

- The document database.
- A set of user profiles, who are to be provided SDI.
- Means with which document description is matched with user description, or simply the computer hardware and software, and
- A user SDI interface.

Document Database

It is the computer aided file of bibliographic records. Like CAS, SDI service may also be provided either from in-house generated databases or from commercially available databases. Both have their own pros and cons. Generally speaking, SDI services provided from in-house databases are time consuming. But at the same time, they are precise and cheaper as that of commercially available SDI services. However, time lag is less in commercially available SDI services.

User Profile

The premier step in designing computerized SDI is to identify the list of users of the library for whom such service is required.

Computer in SDI

Depending up on the population of users, libraries can acquire either stand alone or network based computers for this purpose. However, the large libraries which are mostly connected through LAN, MAN or sometimes even with WAN provide SDI effectively and efficiently. Further, CD-ROM based SDI service is also possible through CD drive or CD Net technology. Sometimes, libraries may develop their own in-house tailor made software to fulfill their specific requirements of SDI. Notably, IIT Kanpur also developed a tailor made or in-house software in the name of iit-KLAS (Kanpur library automation software) to automate its services. Some examples of CD-ROM based SDI services include:

- Single database searching.
- Multi database searching like INSPEC, Chemical Abstracts, LISA, US Patents, etc.

User Interface

This is the mechanism of interaction between the user and the system. It shall positively include:

- Notification to users about the recent literature of their interest.
- Feedback from the users on daily basis.
- Information intermediaries who interact with users and are acknowledgeable concerning databases, retrieval techniques, creation of user profiles, etc. (Richards, 1992).

These services (CAS and SDI) are also sometimes called as alerting information services.

ONLINE SEARCH SERVICES

Online search services or vendors are those organizations which provide online access to a large number of databases over the networked environment and offer search services. Online service means the provision of facilities of online searching of bibliographic and non bibliographic databases using remote terminals. Online searching was primarily used to express the process of openly interrogating the computer systems to determine a particular request for information. However in modern times, online searching is taken to designate the searches that are carried out by means of a local computer that interacts with a remote computer system containing databases.

There are following several components of an online search service:

- Information providers or database developers which offer databases to be accessed in an online mode over the networked environment.
- Vendor or search service supplier. These provide the access to databases and the software to carry out the search.
- Communication links. This links the user of the service with the host and the databases.
- Local workstation. This is a kind of interface via which the user is linked to the service.

Some of the most common examples of online search service are mentioned as under:

- Dialog is the world's leading online search services. It approximately offers online access to over 800 million records in 900 databases in several subjects (http://www.dialog.com).
- OCLC FirstSearch is another globally acknowledged online search services. It offers library users with instant online access to over 72 databases including important databases like OCLC WorldCat, OCLC FirstSearch, Electronic Collections Online, OCLC ArticleFirst etc. (http://www.oclc.org).
- Ovid, an another well known online search service offers access to hundreds of full text journals, renowned textbooks and premier bibliographic databases in many subjects(http://www.ovid.com).
- STN, this online search service offers current and archival information from over 200 scientific,

technical, business and patent databases covering chemistry, engineering, life sciences, pharmaceutical sciences and biotechnology, etc. (http://www.cas.org).

Users for example in DialogWeb can search and retrieve information by using different search modes like Guided search mode and Command search mode. Pertinently, guided search mode does not need knowledge of Dialog's command language. It is planned for the beginners to intermediate searchers. There are two options in guided search facility. The Target search and the Dynamic search. Target search is available in some, but, not all subject categories. It is a readymade search form. On the other hand, Dynamic search is available in all subject categories. It is prepared on the basis of category or databases that are selected. It has access to many more databases than target search and is comparatively flexible. Command search on contrary is prepared for intermediate to experienced searchers. It offers entirely command based access to Dialog's extensive collection of databases. Here users shall be familiar with the several Dialog commands while using command search.

Besides above, there are some examples of online search services that offer access to full text of journals and books. These include:

- EBSCO information service which offers access to huge collection of full text and bibliographic databases appropriate to all types of libraries (http://www.epnet.com).
- Ingenta which offers access to full text of over 5400 publications from over 230 academic and professional publishers (http://www.ingenta.com).
- ProQuest, a resource of electronic collections containing millions of articles primarily appeared in journals, magazines and newspapers etc. (http://proquest.umi.com).

There are many kinds of such online search service such as the traditional super market online search service, specialist online search services, publishers' search services, platform independent services and bibliographic utilities. It may be stated here that some search services offer the users many other benefits such as ease of searching, enhanced processing speed and also affordable prices. In simple words, the automated operations in libraries have made the search services for modern users more specific and user oriented. Notably many reputed and large libraries in India offer such online search services to their bonafide users for the betterment of their research and development and academic excellence.

BIBLIOGRAPHIC SERVICES

The traditional bibliographic services like indexing, abstracting, documentation lists, literature search in bibliographic databases were manual, laborious and undoubtedly time consuming. However, with the development of computer technology followed by their application in libraries, the online bibliographic services became easily possible. Some of the online bibliographic service providers usually subscribed by large libraries for the benefit of their users are:

- Dialog- a worldwide leader in providing online based information services.
- OCLC- Online Computer Library Centre. World Cat is the world's premier online bibliographic service offered by OCLC bibliographic database.
- BLAISE- British Library Automated Information Service. This bibliographic database offers global access to major British Library catalogues and other notable UK bibliographic databases.
- ESA-IRS- The European Space Agency Information Retrieval Service offers complete scientific and technical aerospace information online (Saffady, 1989).

It may be mentioned here that these online bibliographic service providers are on subscription in many large Indian academic libraries. Some of the examples of external bibliographic services subscribed by Indian libraries for their users include:

Ei Compendex

This provides gists of technical reports, journal articles, conference papers, etc., on engineering and technology.

Current Contents Search

An electronic version of Current Contents is greatly acknowledged current awareness tool from ISI (USA).

INSPEC

A leading database of the world in the fields of physics, electronics and electrical engineering, computers and control and information technology. This database is looked after by Institute of Electrical Engineers (IEE), USA. The other commercially available bibliographic services are Biological Abstracts, Chemical Abstracts and LISA, etc. All these online search services are commonly taken for information retrieval in modern days.

DOCUMENT DELIVERY SERVICES

In traditional libraries, document delivery services were taken as the bibliographic information services provided to the users, generally with reference to books with or without abstracts. But, this service was mostly time consuming and at times had lost its relevance till it reached the destination. However like other services, the automated libraries made this service fast, accurate and in a better and cheaper way over networked environment. In automated environment, this service better known as electronic document delivery service is the transfer of information/document from library to a borrower by electronic mechanism such as videotext, email or on CD-ROM. It is sometimes also called as CD-ROM service of the library. Simply, electronic document delivery service refers to the use of electronic technologies in providing inter library lending activities. The electronic document delivery service according to Braid (1993) shall meet the following steps:

- The identification of information/document to be delivered.
- Locating the source where such information/ document is contained.
- Requesting/if the document is not available in the parent library.
- The processing in between the parent library and the library where the document is available and between the end user to whom document/ information is to be delivered.
- Delivering/supplying the document.
- Receiving the document by the user.
- Feedback from the receiver/user.

It is pertinent to point out here that all these steps are carried out in networked environment. In providing such electronic documents/information to users, there would be some infrastructural requirements which include Web server, Web browser, scanner and laser printer. E-mail systems, online union catalogues, teletype and telefascimile are modern means of electronic document delivery services. In this direction, many Indian libraries with special mention of those attached with Defense Research and Development Organization (DRDO), Defense Science Information and Documentation Centre (DESIDOC), Indian Space Research Organizations (ISRO), Baba Atomic Research Centre (BARC) and the like organizations are provided such electronic document delivery to their users (scientists) very fast. Some technological libraries have also started such services to their users. However, Indian academic libraries are mostly yet to start such automated document delivery to their users. Nevertheless, large Indian libraries are delivering their bonafide users with their relevant information through emails on request.

COMPUTERIZED INDEXES

Printed indexes are one of the premier applications of the computerized information retrieval services. Pertinently, computers were applied for the preparation of in-house indexes to reports, in-house abstracting and indexing bulletins, patent lists, etc., and also for the preparation for indexing of some of the key abstracting journals such as Chemical Abstracts, Biological Abstracts, etc. In the present days, indexes have become one of the series of database products. These indexes generally comprise of series of lead terms arranged usually in alphabetical order. Computerized indexes majorly rely on automatically assigned index terms. They can also be based on intellectually assigned terms. There are many kinds of computer generated index terms. Of these kinds, one is the keyword based indexes. This category of computer generated indexes includes the following indexes:

- KWIC (Keyword in Context Index).
- KWOC (Keyword out of context Index).
- KWAC (Keyword Augmented Index).
- KWIT (Keyword in Title Index).

All these computer generated indexes are based on keywords, nevertheless they are differently formatted (Galhotra, 2008).

CITATION INDEXES

Computers can also generate effective index by means of citation indexing for arranging and reformatting entries. The input to this indexing system includes the references of latest articles brought out in some of the key journals in any subject field. For each article, a citation index lists cited documents alongwith the list of citing articles. One of the best examples of citation indexes is that of Science Citation Index developed first by Eugene Garfield in the Institute of Scientific Information (ISI) at Philadelphia, USA. The vitality of this index is that in a given cited document in a subject field, the user should be in position to trace the other relevant items. It may be mentioned here that citation links offer an important added approach to the detection of related items. This kind of indexing is possible mainly through the application of computers in indexing (Galhotra, 2008).

CD-ROM DATABASE PRODUCTS AND SERVICES

CD-ROM uses the digital audio compact disc system for storage and retrieval of machine readable information. Optical storage technology uses the optical scanning techniques for storing huge information in a compact area. In the present world of information storage and retrieval, optical discs particularly CD-ROMS have become important medium for storage and dissemination of information. They are also used as an alternative method for online access to external databases subscribed by a particular library. Take the example of a document like Encyclopedia Britannica which is available in a full text in a compact disc, it can be searched any number of times at any place with the facility to copy a part of it for further use by other users. On the other hand, such facility was not possible in the physical form of same Encyclopedia Britannica. In the modern automated libraries, the services of providing CD-ROMS for many sources are available in Indian libraries. These services are popularizing with each passing day in Indian libraries.

AUTOMATED REFERENCE SERVICES

Gone are the days when reference services were entirely considered as the services provided with personal touch by the librarians to the readers. Now, reference services are computer aided with user at some other place and services being delivered in a virtual networked environment. Towards the decades of 60s and 70s, many libraries procured computer aided bibliographic and non-bibliographic databases for processing on in-house computers using locally developed information retrieval software. However, most of the libraries of that era were short of hardware and software infrastructure. Nevertheless through early 70s, charge based search services in libraries became possible by the producers of machine readable databases. It was in the mid-70s that the services provided via offline batch processing mode were taken over by online database searching. Now, these online search services are widely used by the libraries and are divided into two groups according to saffdy (1989). They comprise multidisciplinary services and specialized services. Multidisciplinary services include:

- DIALOG,
- BRS,
- ORBIT,
- WILSONLINE,
- DATASTAR, and
- ESAIRS.

These online search services offer database coverage of many different subjects for the users. The other specialized services include:

- NLM Search service,
- STN international,
- Lexis, and
- WESTLAW.

These types of online search services offer online access to one or more databases pertaining to an individual subject, profession like medicine, law, engineering, etc. (Saffady, 1989). It is worth noting here that many Indian libraries both special and academic provide these online search services to their bonafide users. However, these kinds of services are more vibrant in libraries attached with research and development organizations than academic libraries, though large university libraries also provide some of these services to their noted clienteles.

AUTOMATED LIBRARY SERVICES AWARENESS

The maximum and effective utilization of automated library systems has a direct relationship of users' awareness with them. The more the users' are aware and technically skilled, the more utilization of automated services of a particular library will flourish. Since the users of technological institutions are exposed to many software applications including library automation softwares as a part of their curriculum, they are supposedly to be more aware about the automated services provided through library softwares as compared to the users of other institutions. It is obvious that this learned community will have more awareness about the automated services of their respective libraries. On the other hand, it has been seen that majority of users in Indian academic libraries at college level are not aware about the various automated services. While at university level, this number of users is higher, since many universities have automated their libraries.

Even though a large number of users in Indian universities are using automated library services, but, a considerable percentage is still away from taking the benefits of these wonderful automated library services. To some extent, this may owe to the fact that the users are directly dealing with the OPAC and other search and retrieval services of a particular library, while some of the automated services goes unutilized. In this connection, the onus lies on the librarians to conduct various training and orientation courses for acquainting their users about various wonderful automated services. Besides, libraries can also promote their automated services and their wonderful benefits through mass media and local newspapers. This will not only make a good publicity of library services among the learned society, but will also help in garnering more interest among the new users towards libraries. It is worth mentioning here that many Indian libraries with special reference to IIT libraries and some special libraries of research and development organizations offer the awareness of automated services of their libraries through many modern means and modes.

SATISFACTION WITH THE SERVICES OF AUTOMATED LIBRARY SYSTEM

Now-a-days, there is a growing trend among Indian university libraries and reputed college libraries for automating their library system by installing integrated library management systems that are compatible to all international standards. However, the effectiveness and success of any library system does not merely depend on the implementation of these integrated library systems, but upon the satisfaction of users with the system in place. In this respect, an indigenous survey surfaced in 2013 and revealed that 85% students, 87% research scholars and 92% faculty members in IIT Delhi are either strongly satisfied or satisfied with the overall services of automated library system. This number of users has been found somewhat similar in IIT Kanpur; where 85% students, 86% research scholars and 87% faculty members are also strongly satisfied or satisfied in this regard. It may be mentioned here that these IIT libraries are using LibSys integrated library management package which is popularly used by large number of Indian libraries. Surprisingly the automated library system of Kashmir University, as against these IIT libraries, has been found better as more number of users with 89% students, 97% research scholars and 96% faculty members are either strongly satisfied or satisfied with the automated services of their library system. Kashmir University library is using one of the leading international library package i.e. Virtua.

Notwithstanding the fact that automation has enhanced the library services to a greater extent, some users, even if smaller in number are dissatisfied with the automated library system of IIT libraries, though they use a standard LibSys library software package. The scenario is a bit different in Kashmir University where few users have expressed their dissatisfaction with their automated library system.

It is worth stating here that a majority of users in these libraries have shown their satisfaction with the services of their respective automated library system. Amazingly, this number has been found more in Kashmir University than the IITs. Pertinently, the automated library system has speeded up the promptness of library services. In this system, users can approach the in-charge of cataloguing section for their requested book, who within a short span of time through automated acquisition module can generate the catalogue, book label and bar-code for the procured book and forward it immediately to the circulation counter for users.

Similarly, users can also request the staff at serials section counter for a list of holdings of foreign journals. The staff can immediately generate the desired list with the help of printer attached with the computer terminal in the serials control module. Needless to point out here that automated circulation system saved a lot of time, as the books are now quickly issued and returned by using bar code readers against the smart RFID cards. It is also notable to mention here that users need not to wait in long queues which were seen earlier at manual circulation counter, as they can now issue and return the books by their own through self check-out and check-in systems facility available in the automated library system.

As a part of suggestions for the betterment of a library system, a printing facility should also be made available in order to get print outs for the search results. At least one printer can be attached on OPAC terminal for this purpose. A vibrant help desk, besides online reference librarian is also advisable so that the queries of users particularly short reference ones are addressed without wasting precious time of users. Indian librarians should also seriously think over online reference service, which is a common feature of most of the American and European libraries. Though some Indian libraries mention on their websites the availability of Ask the Librarian facility, but practically this service does not work to the required extent.

During the selection committees, the aspirants possessing proficiency in managing the automated library systems and integrated library packages to satisfy the heterogeneous needs of modern techno oriented users at their desktops shall be given added advantage with extra incentives over other candidates.

In order to inculcate the better understanding of modern library management systems for the effective use of library resources to garner the research and development enthusiasm among the students at an early age, the education policy needs to be revisited and Library and Information Science discipline with greater emphasis on library automation is suggested to be taught at college and secondary school levels in India.

REFERENCES

Braid, J. Andrew (1993). Electronic Document Delivery: A Reality at Last? *ASLIB Proceedings*. 45 (6), 161-166.

Galhotra, M.K. (2008). *Information Technology in Library and Information Services*. New Delhi : ESS ESS, pp. 151-159.

Hilal, A., & Mehtab, A.A. (2016). *Library Automation in India : An Evaluative Study*. New Delhi : Ane Books, pp. 134-135.

Kemp, A. (1979). *Current Awareness Services*. London: Clive Bingley

Kreslins, K., O'Brein, A., & Smith, I. A. (1994). Online Public Access Catalogues in Latvia: Strategies for Subject Access. *International Information and Library Review*, 26, 31-50.

Luhn, H. P. (1961). Selective Dissemination of New Scientific Information with the Aid of Electronic Processing. *American Documentation.* 12 (4), 133-138.

Peake, D. G. (1981) Library Automation in Australia; The State of Art. *Program Automated Library and Information Systems*, 15(1), 11-23.

Richards, D. (1992). Dissemination of Information. In. *Handbook of Special Librarianship and Information Work.* ASLIB: London.

Sajjad ur Rehman., & Reham, A. (2010). Integrated Systems Applications in Kuwait Academic Libraries. *The Electronic Library*, 28(6), 858-872.

Saffady, W. (1989). Library Automation: An Overview. *Library Trends*, 37(3), 273-277.

http://proquest.umi.com/pqdweb

http://www.cas.org/stnonline.html

http://www.dialog.com/about/

http://www.dialog.com

http://www.epnet.com/default.asp

http://www.ingenta.com/

http://www.ntis.gov/search.htm

http://www.oclc.org/firstsearch/

http://www.oclc.org/oclc/menu/home1.htm

Suggested Readings

BOOKS

Adams, R. J. (1986). *Information Technology and Libraries: A Future for Academic Libraries*. London: Croom Helem.

Ahmad, S. (2003). *Computer in Library Management.* New Delhi: APH.

Agarwal, U. K. (Ed.). (2004). *Computer Applications to Library and Information Science*. Udaipur: Ankur Prakashan.

Amudhavalli, A. (Ed.). (2008). *Dynamics in Digital Information Systems (Festschrift Volume in Honour of Prof. M. Bavakutty)*. New Delhi: ESS ESS.

Anandan, C., & Gangathanan, M. (Eds.). (2006). *Digital Libraries from Technology to Culture*. New Delhi: Kanishka.

Aswal, R.S. (2003). *CDS/ISIS for Windows: A Handbook for Librarians*. New Delhi: ESS ESS.

Aswal, R.S. (2006). *Library Automation for 21st Century*. New Delhi: ESS ESS.

Babu, A. T., & Ramiaha, L. S. (Eds.). (2006). *Developing Cyber Libraries*. New Delhi : Allied.

Baby, M. D., Reghunathan, R., & Stanly, J. P. (Eds.). (2000). *Changing Trends in Library and Information Science*. New Delhi: ESS ESS.

Bajirjian, R. (1995). *New Automation Technology for Acquisitions and Collection Development.* New York: The Haworth Press.

Balakrishnan, S. (2000). *Networking and the Future of Libraries*. New Delhi: ESS ESS.

Balakrishnan, S., & Palival, P. K. (2001). *Library Collections and Automation*. New Delhi: Anmol.

Balakrishnan, Shyama., & P. K. Palival (Ed.). (2001). *Contemporary Information Technology Scenario.* New Delhi: Anmol.

Bavakutty, M., Mohammed, S. T. K., & Mohamed, H. K. (Eds.). (2006). *Research on Library Computerization.* New Delhi: Authors Press.

Bilal, D. (2002). *Automating Media Centers and Small Libraries: A Micro Computer-Based Approach.* (2nd ed.). Colorado: Libraries Unlimited.

Boss, R. W. (1982). *Automating Library Acquisitions: Issues and Outlook.* London: Knowledge Industry.

Boss, R. W. (1990). *The Library Manager's Guide to Automation.* Boston: G. K. Hall.

Bridges, K. (Ed.). (2003). *Expectations of Librarians in the 21st century.* London: Greenwood Press.

Brophy, P. (2007). *The Library in the Twenty First Century.* (2nd Ed.). London: Facet.

Buragohain, A., & Baisya, K. N. (Eds.). (1994). *Librarianship and Information Technology.* New Delhi: Osmans.

Burns, A. (Ed.). (1984). *New Information Technology.* England: Ellis Horwood.

Busha, C. H., & Stephen P. H. (1980). *Research Methods in Librarianship: Techniques & Interpretation.* New York: Academic Press.

Cash, J. I., Eccles, R. G., Nohria, N., & Nolan, R. L. (1994). *Building the Information Age Organization: Structure, Control & Information Technologies.* Homewood, IL: Irwin

Cauvery, R., Nayak, S. U. K., Girja, M., & Meenakshi, R. (2003). *Research Methodology for Students of Social Sciences.* New Delhi: S. Chand.

Chand A. S. (Ed.). (2011). Integrated Library System Design and Development Approaches. In *Knowledge Management in Digital Era.* New Delhi : Westville.

Chandra, R., & Anand, P. S. (Eds.). (2003). *Technological Changes in Libraries.* Delhi: Kalpaz.

Chaudhary, S. K. (2002). *Modern Library Strategies.* New Delhi: APH.

Clayton, M., & Batt C. (1992). *Managing Library Automation.* Hants, England: Ashgate.

Cohn, J. M. (1998). *Planning for Library Automation.* London: Library Association.

Cohn, J. M., Kelsey, A. L., & Fiels, K. M. (2002). *Planning for Library Automation: A how-to-do-it Manual for Librarians.* London: Facet.

Cohn, J. M., Kelsey, A. L., & Fiels, K. M. (2002). *Planning for Integrated Systems and Technologies: a how-to-do-it Manual for Libraries.* London: Facet.

Contractor, M. (1998). *Computer and Library Services.* New Delhi: Anmol.

Cooper, M. D. (1996). *Design of Library Automation Systems: File Structures, Data Structures and Tools.* New York: John Wiley and Sons.

Cope, B., & Angus, P. (2006). *The Future of the Book in Digital Age.* Oxford: Chandos.

Corbin, J. (1985). *Managing the Library Automation Project.* Phoenix, AZ : Oryx.

Cortez, E. M., & Smorch, T. (1993). *Planning Second Generation Automated Library Systems.* Westport, CT: Greenwood Press.

Craghill, D., Neale C., & Wilson, T. D. (1989). *The Impact of IT on Staff Development in UK Public Libraries.* London: British Library Board.

Cyganski, D., John, A. O., & Richard, F. V. (2001). *Information Technology Inside and Outside.* New Jersey: Prentice Hall.

Das, B. (2007). *Current Tools and Techniques in Library Science.* New Delhi: Cyber Tech.

Das, S. R. (2008). *Library Automation and Information Technology.* New Delhi: Arise.

Deewan, B. (2002). *Managing Information Technology.* New Delhi: Vikas.

Devarajan, G., & Rahelamma, A. V. (1990). *Library Computerization in India.* Isaac Festschrift Papers Presented in Honour of Prof. K.A. Isaac. New Delhi: ESS ESS.

Devarajan, G. (Ed.). (1996). *Progress in Information Technology.* New Delhi: ESS ESS.

Devarajan, G. (1999). *Information Technology in Libraries.* New Delhi: ESS ESS.

Duval, B. K., & Main, L. (1992). *Automated Library Systems: A librarian's Guide and Teaching Manual.* Westport, CT: Meckler.

Dyer, H., & Morris, A. (1990). *Human Aspects of Library Automation.* Hants, England: Gower.

Fayen, E. G. (1983). *The Online Catalogue: Improving Public Access to Library Materials.* White Plains, NY: Knowledge Industry.

Fenner, A. (Ed.). (2005). *Managing Digital Resources in Libraries.* New York: The Haworth Press.

Fresko, M., & Lynne, B. (1992). *Optical Disc Technology and European Libraries: A Case Study of User and Technical Requirements.* London: Bowker Saur.

Godden, I. P. (Ed.). (1984). *Library Technical Services: Operations and Management.* Orlando: Academic Press.

Goode, W. J., & Paul, K. H. (2006). *Methods in Social Research.* Delhi: Surjeet.

Gopal, K., Shyama., & Palival, P. K. (2000). *Library Online Cataloguing in Digital Way.* Delhi: Authors Press.

Gopal, K. (2001). *Intellectual Freedom in Digital Libraries.* Delhi: Authors Press.

Gorman, M. (1998). *Technical Services Today & Tomorrow.* Colorado: Libraries Unlimited.

Grosch, A. N. (1995). *Library Information Technology and Networks.* New York: Marcel Dekker.

Gupta, S. P. (Ed.). (1993). *Information Technology and Health Science Libraries.* New Delhi: Medical Library Association of India.

Gupta, S. P. (1995). *Manpower Needs of Automated Libraries.* New Delhi: ESS ESS.

Hagler, R., & Simmons, P. (1982). *The Bibliographic Record and Information Technology.* Chicago: American Library Association.

Haravu, L. J. (2004). *Library Automation: Design, Principles and Practice.* New Delhi: Allied.

Head, J. W., & McCabe, G. B. (Eds.). (1993). *Insiders Guide to Library Automation.* Westport, CT: Greenwood Press.

Head, J. W., & McCabe, G. B. (1996). *Introducing and Managing Academic Library Automation Projects.* Westport: Greenwood Press.

Heiliger, E. M., & Paul, B. H. (1970). *Library Information Systems: From Library Automation to Distributed Information Access Solutions.* Westport: Libraries Unlimited.

Heiliger, E. M., & Paul, B. H. (1971). *Library Automation; Experience, Methodology and Technology of Library Information System.* New York: McGraw Hill.

Helgesen, S. (1995). *The Web of Inclusion.* New York: Doubleday.

Herring, J., & Mackenzie, J. A. (1986). *Planning for Library Automation; Aberdeen City Libraries.* London: Library Association.

Hewitt, J. A. (Ed.). (1988). *Advances in Library Automation and Networking.* London: JAI Press.

Houghton FLA, B. (Ed.). (1968). *Computer Based Information Retrieval Systems.* London: Clive Bingley.

Howard, N. (2005). *The Book: The Life Story of a Technology.* Westport, Connecticut: Greenwood Press.

Iyer, V. K. (1999). *Library Information Technology Tools of Tomorrow.* Delhi : Rajat.

Jeevan, V. K. J. (2006). *Computers @ Libraries.* New Delhi: ESS ESS.

Johnson, E. D. (1965). *A History of Libraries in the Western World.* New York: The Scare Crow.

Johnson, P. (1991). *Automation and Organizational Change in Libraries.* Boston: G. K. Hall.

Kanakachary, M. (1996). *Towards Networking of Humanities Libraries in India.* New Delhi: ESS ESS.

Kashyap, M. M. (2006). *Computer Based Library Information System Designing Techniques.* Bangalore: Sarda Ranganathan Endowment for Library Science.

Kaul, H. K. (1992). *Library Networks: An Indian Experience.* New Delhi : Virgo.

Kaushal, M. (Ed.). (1995). *Library Science and Information Technology: Modern Library Science Services-7.* New Delhi: Common Wealth.

Kiesler, S., & Sproull, L. (Eds.). (1987). *Computing and Change on Campus.* Cambridge, MA: Cambridge University Press.

Kimber, R. T. (1974). *Automation in Libraries.* (2nd ed.). Oxford: Pergamon Press.

Kochar, R. S., & Sudarshan, K. N. (1997). *Library Automation Issues and Systems.* New Delhi: APH.

Kochtanek, T. R., & Joseph, R. M. (2004). *Library Information Systems; From Library Automation to Distributed Information Access Solutions.* Westport: Libraries Unlimited.

Kothari, C. R. (2004). *Research Methodology Methods & Techniques.* New Delhi: New Age International.

Kuldeep, C. (Ed.). (1993). *Current Trends in Information Technology: Its Impact on Information Science in India.* New Delhi: Batra.

Kumar, P. S. G. (1987). *Computerization in Indian Libraries.* Delhi: B. R. Publishing.

Kumar, S. (2009). *Some Perspectives of Integrated Library Systems.* New Delhi: Rajat.

Lane, E. S. (1990). *Micro Computer Management and Maintenance for Libraries.* London: Meckler.

Lioyd, L. (Ed.). (1992). *Campus-Wide Information Systems and Networks: Case Studies in Design and Implementation.* London: Meckler.

Lovecy, I. (1984). *Automating Library Procedures; A Survivor's Handbook.* New Delhi: D. K. Agencies.

Lynden, F. C. (Ed.). (2001). *Advances in Librarianship.* San Diego: Academic Press.

Madan, S. (1987). *Computer & Library Services.* Delhi: Commonwealth.

Mahapatra, P. K. (1985). *The Computer in Library Services.* Calcutta. The World Press.

Mahapatra, P. K., & Chakrabarti, B. (1997). *Redesigning the Library.* New Delhi: ESS ESS.

Mahapatra, P. K., & Chakrabarti, B. (2000). *Book Byte and Beyond: Library Without Walls.* New Delhi: ESS ESS.

Malavya, V. C. (1999). *Library Information Technology for the Next Millennium.* New Delhi: ESS ESS.

Malwad, N. M., Rajeshkar, T. B., Rao, R. I. K., & Satyanarayana, N. V. (Eds.). (1996). *Digital Libraries Dynamics Storehouse of Digitized Information.* New Delhi: New Age International.

Marsterson, W. (1986). *Information Technology and the Role of Librarian.* London: Croom Helm.

Massis, B. E. (2004). *The Practical Library Trainer.* New York: The Haworth Press.

Mathews, J. R. (Ed.). (1983). *A Reader on Choosing and Automated Library System.* Chicago: American Library Association.

Mcleod, J., & Catherine, H. (Eds.). (2005). *Managing Electronic Records.* London: Facet.

Mehatab, D. (2008). *Infotech@Library Services.* Delhi: Authors Press.

Mittal, S. (2005). *Modern Library Administration and Automation.* New Delhi: ESS ESS.

Moodgal, H. M. K., & Kokila, K. G. (2000). *CD-ROM Technology Librarians' Info Guide*. Delhi: Author Press.

Morris, A. (1992). *The Application of Expert Systems in Libraries and Information Centers*. London: Bowker-Saur.

Mott, T. H. (Jr.)., Susan, A., & Levy, S. (1972). *Introduction to PL/I Programming for Library and Information Science*. New York: Academic Press.

Mount, E. (Ed.). (1988). *Adaptation of Turnkey Computer Systems in Sci-Tech Libraries*. New York: The Haworth Press.

Mukhopadhyay, A. K. (1996). *Microprocessor Microcomputer and their Applications*. New Delhi: Narosa.

Nair, R. R. (1992). *Computer Applications to Library and Information Services*. New Delhi: ESS ESS.

Nair, R. R. (1995). *Academic Library Automation: Perspectives in Academic Librarianship-3*. New Delhi: ESS ESS.

Oliver, P. (2008). *Writing Your Theses*. (2nd Ed). New Delhi: Sage.

Padmajan, C. K. (2002). *Essentials of Automated Acquisition*. New Delhi: ESS ESS.

Palmer, M. (2009). *Making the Most of RFID in Libraries*. London: Facet.

Panigrahi, R. M. (2000). *Impact of Information Technology on Libraries*. New Delhi: ESS ESS.

Parnami, A. (2007). *Integrated Libraries and Information Systems*. New Delhi: Cyber Tech.

Parthasarathy, R. (Ed.). (1986). *Computer Application to Libraries, I R and Networking*. Bangalore: Sarda Ranganathan Endowment for Library Science.

Paruthi, S. N. (Ed.). (1997). *Library Techniques and Technologies: Perspectives in Multimedia Library Development*. New Delhi: Kanishka.

Patil, D. B. (1991). *Dbase III Plus in Libraries and Information Centers: Theory and Practice*. New Delhi: Ashish.

Patterson, D. W. (2009). *Introduction to Artificial Intelligence and Expert Systems*. New Delhi: PHI Learning.

Peters, T. A. (1991). *The Online Catalog: A Critical Examination of Public Use*. Jefferson, N: McFarland.

Pickard, A. J. (2007). *Research Methods in Information*. London: Facet.

Pitkin, G. M. (Ed.). (1991). *The Evolution of Library Automation;*

Management Issues and Future Perspectives. Westport: Meckler.

Prasher, R. G. (1991). *India's University Libraries; Organizations, Operations and Services.* Ludhiana: Medallion.

Prasher, R. G. (Ed.). (2003). *Indian Libraries in IT Environment.* Ludhiana: Medallion Press.

Rakesh, L. B. (2006). *Library & Information Science in Digital Age.* New Delhi: Alfa.

Ramalingam (Ed.). (2000). *Library and Information Technology: Concepts to Applications.* Delhi: Kalpaz.

Rao, P. V. S. (2005). *Library and Information Technology.* New Delhi: Sonali.

Reddy, P. S. (2001). *Automated Management of Library Collection.* New Delhi: ESS ESS.

Reitz, J. M. (2004). *Dictionary of Library and Information Science.* Westport: Libraries Unlimited.

Reynolds, D. (1985). *Library Automation Issues and Applications.* New York: R. R. Bowker.

Rhyno, A. (2004). *Using Open Source Systems for Digital Libraries.* Westport, London: Libraries Unlimited.

Riaz, M. (1992). *Library Automation.* New Delhi: Atlantic.

Rodda, L. J. (1985). *Managing Information in the Electronic Office.* Virginia: Reston.

Rowley, J. E. (1987). *Organizing Knowledge: An Introduction to Information Retrieval.* England: Gower.

Rowley, J. E. (1993). *Computers for Libraries.* London: Library Association.

Saffady, W. (1983). *Introduction to Automation for Librarians.* Chicago: ALA.

Jagdesh, S., & Mahesh, V. M. (1998). *Library Automation Using Foxpro 2.0.* New Delhi: ESS ESS.

Salmon, S. R. (Ed). (1969). *Library Automation: A State of Art Review.* Chicago: American Library Association.

Salmon, S. R. (1975). *Library Automation Systems.* New York: Marcel Dekkar.

Samuel, T. M., & Mani, S. (2008). *Internet and Information Technology.* New Delhi: Commonwealth.

Satyanarayana, B., Babu, R. B., Reddy, V. P., & Babu, A. T. (Eds.).

(1998). *Information Technology: Issues and Trends (Festschrift in Honour of Prof. N. Guruswamy Naidu).* New Delhi: Cosmo.

Satyanarayana, N. R. (2003). *A Manual of Library Automation and Networking.* Lucknow: New Royal Book.

Sehgal, R. L., & Behl, P. K. (1996). *Manual on Computer Applications Training in Library Science.* New Delhi: ESS ESS.

Sehgal, R. L. (1998). *User Education in Computer Based Libraries.* New Delhi: ESS ESS.

Sehgal, R. L. (1998). *Handbook of Library Software Packages.* New Delhi: ESS ESS.

Sehgal, R. L. (2000). *Intranet and Internet Applications for Librarians.* New Delhi: ESS ESS.

Sharma, C. K., & Jain, M. K. (2008). *Research Methodology.* New Delhi: Shree Publishers.

Sharma, P. S. K. (1993). *Library Computerization Theory & Practice.* New Delhi: ESS ESS.

Sharma, P. S. K. (1995). *Fundamentals of Library Automation with Illustrations.* New Delhi: ESS ESS.

Singh, S. K. (2000). *Library Technical Services Millennium Approach.* Delhi: Author press.

Singh, S. K. (2002). *Essentials of Integrated Library Management.* Delhi: Author press.

Singh, U. N. (2004). *Information Technology in Libraries.* New Delhi: Shree Publishers.

Sinnot, H. F., & Sinnot, L. T. (1983). *The Electronic Library: The Impact of Automation on Academic Libraries.* Lexington Mass: Lexington Books.

Swihart, S., & Hefley, B. F. (1973). *Computer Systems in the Library: A Handbook for Managers & Designers.* California: Melville.

Tariq, A. (2004). *Library Services in an Electronic Environment.* New Delhi: Kaveri Books.

Thapa, N. (2007). *Slices of Library Automation.* Agra: YK.

Toohil, B. G. (1980). *Guide to Library Automation.* Mclean: MITRE.

Tyagi, S. (Ed.). (2001). *Modern Trends in Libraries.* New Delhi: Rajat.

Vasanth, N., & Mudhol, M. V. (2000). *Software Packages for Library Automation.* New Delhi: ESS ESS.

Venketaramana, P. (2004). *Information Technology Applications in Libraries.* New Delhi: ESS ESS.

Venkatapiah, V. F. (Ed.). (1994). *New Horizons in Library and Information Science.* Madras: TR.

Vittal, N., & Mahalingam, S. (2001). *Information Technology: India's Tomorrow.* New Delhi: Manas.

Wilson, T. L. (Ed.). (2003). *The Twenty First Century Art Librarian.* New York: The Haworth Press.

Webb, T. D. (1987). *The In-House Option: Professional Issues of Library Automation.* New York: The Haworth Press.

Woodsworth, A. (1991). *Patterns and Options for Managing Information Technology on Campus.* Chicago, IL: American Library Association.

Zuboff, S. (1988). *In the Age of Smart Machine.* New York: Basic Books.

JOURNALS

Albanese, A. R. (2004). Campus Library 2.0. *Library Journal,* 30-33.

Ali, A. (1995, May). Computerizing University Libraries. *University News: A Weekly Journal of Higher Education,* New Delhi: Association of Indian Universities. 9-11.

Alley, B. (1988). Reshaping Technical Services for Effective Staff Utilization. *Journal of Library Administration,* 9(1), 105-110.

Atkinson, H. (1975). Personal Savings through Computerized Library System. *Library Trends,* 23(4), 587-594.

Babu, B. R., & O'Brein, A. (2000). Web OPAC Interfaces: An Overview. *The Electronic Library,* 18(5), 316-330.

Battin, P. (1984). The Electronic Library: A Vision for the Future. *Educom Bulletin,* 19(2), 12-17.

Bednar, M. (1988). Automation of Cataloguing. *Journal of Academic Librarianship,* 14(3), 145-149.

Bevis, M. D., & McCabe, S. (1994). NOTIS as an Impetus for Change in Technical Services Departmental Staffing. *Technical Services Quarterly,* 12, 29-43.

Bocher, B. (1993). Small Automated Library Systems. *Computers in Libraries,* 13, 26.

Bock, D. K. (1985). From Libraries to Learning Resources: Six Decades of Progress-and Still Changing. *Community & Junior College Libraries,* 3(2), 35-45.

Borgman, C. L. (1997). From Acting Locally to Thinking Globally: A

Brief History of Library Automation. *Library Quarterly*, 67(3), 215-249.

Brindley, L. (2005). British Library and e-Learning. *IFLA Journal*, 31(1), 13-18.

Busch, B. J. (1985). Automation and Reorganization of Technical and Public Services. *SPEC flyer*, 112.

Butcher, R. (1993). An Overview of British Library Automation at St. Pancras. *Program*, 27(3), 281-292.

Carpenter, B. (1998). Your Attention Please! Marketing Today's Libraries. *Computers in Libraries*, 18(8), 62-66.

Cheney, H. (1993). Administration and Management: Library Automation Systems Project. *Library Software Review*, 12, 6-22.

C. L. Systems. (1981). C. L. Systems Holds Commanding Lead Among Circulation Systems Marketers. *Advanced Technology Libraries*, 10, 1-7.

Combs, J. (1995). Total Library Computerization, Version 2: A DOS-Based Program from On Point, Inc., for Managing Small to Midsized Libraries. *Library Software Review, 14*(3), 185-199.

Condous, C. (1983). Cost-Benefit Analysis and the Implementation of Automated Systems. *LAISE*, 14(2), 2-8.

Cotta, M. V. (1989). Automation and Academic Library Structure. *Libri*, 39(1), 47- 63.

Dada, G. (1999). Computer Networking in National libraries. *Lagos Librarian*, 20(1&2), 1-5

Dakashinamurti, G. (1985). Automation's Effect on Library Personnel. *Canadian Librarian Journal*, 42, 343-351.

Daniels, R. J. (1995). Effects on Non-professional Staff of the Implementation of Computer Based Library Systems in College Libraries: Some Case Studies. *Program*, 29(1), 1-13.

De Gennaro, R. (1976, Jan). Library Automation: Changing Patterns and New Directions. *Library Journal*, 101(1), 175-183.

Dennis, N. K., Carter, C. E., & Bordeianu, S. (1997). Vision vs Reality: Planning for the Implementation of a Web Based Online Catalogue in an Academic Library. *Library HiTech, 15(3-4), 159-170.*

Dorman, D. (2002). OCLC Taps VTLS to help Migrate Worldcat. *American Libraries*, 33(5), 83.

Dover, M. (1993). Review of Issues in the Use of Library Automation.

Library Management, 14, 78-90.

Druschel, J. (1981). Cost Analysis of an Automated and Manual Cataloguing and Book Processing Systems. *Journal of Library Automation*, 14(1), 24-29.

Dwyer, J. R. (1988). The Evolutionary Role of Technical Services. *Journal of Library Administration*, 9(1), 13-26.

Elman, S. S. (1991). Automation in U.S. East Asian Libraries in the United States: A Review and Assessment. *College & Research Libraries*, 52(6), 559-573.

Epstein, S. B. (1983). Suddenly Last Decade: Automation Arrives. *Library Journal*, 108 (X), 183-185.

Evans, M. E. (1979). University of York Library Automation Project. *Program*, 13(2), 85- 105.

Fayllot, J. (1972). On-line Serials Control System in a Large Biomedical Library. *Journal for American Society for Information Science*, 318- 322.

Feret, B., & Marcinek, M. (1999). The Future of Academic Library and Academic Librarian: A Delphi Study. *Librarian Career Development*, 7(10), 91.

Fox, R. (1999). Tomorrow's Library Today. *Association for Computing Machinery: Communications of the ACM*, 40(1), 20-21.

Garcha, R., & Butler, L. J. (1996). Profiling African Libraries; Automation in Ghana, Kenya and Nigeria. *Library Review*, 45 (6), 25-35.

Ghosh, T. K., & Panda, K. C. (2011). Automated Serials Control at the Indian Institute of Technology: An Overview. *Program: Electronic Library and Information Systems*, 45(2), 173-184.

Gomes, S. R. (2004). Virtual Library: A New Territory for Scientific Research in Brazil. *The International Information & Library Review*, 36, 13-21.

Gorman, M. (1979). On Doing Away with Technical Services Departments. *American Libraries*, 10, 435-437.

Grosch, A. N. (1976). Library Automation. *Annual Review of Information Science and Technology*, 11, 225-265.

Hallmark, J., & Garcia, R. (1996). Training for Automated Systems in Libraries. *Information Technology & Libraries*, 15(3), 157-168.

Harrington, S. A. (1986). The Changing Environment in Technical Services. *Technical Services Quarterly*, 4(2), 7-20.

Harrison, K., & Summers, D. (1988). Development of an Automated Acquisition System at the University of Lancaster Library. *Program,* 22(2), 143-162.

Hegarty, K. (1985). Myths of Library Automation. *Library Journal,* 110(16), 43-49.

Hewitt, J. A. (1976). The Impact of OCLC. *American Libraries,* 7(5), 268- 275.

Hoffman, E. (1988). Managing Automation. *Library HiTech,* 6(1), 45-54.

Holley, R. P. (1981). The Future of Cataloguing and Cataloguers. *Journal of Academic Librarianship,* 7(2), 90-93.

Horney, K. L. (1987). Fifteen Years of Automation: Evolution of Technical Services Staffing. *Library Resources and Technical Services,* 31, 69-76.

Idowu, A. O. (2000). Ready-Made Software for Nigerian Libraries' Automation Projects: A Survey of Existing Facilities. *Lagos Librarian,* 21(1&2), 38-45.

Iskandarani, A. I., & Anwar, M. A. (1992). Automated Bilingual Circulation System Using PC Local Area Networks. *Micro Computers for Information Management,* 9(3), 161-176.

Jaramillo, G. R. (1988). Computer Technology and its Impact on Collection Development. *Collection Management,* 10(1/2), 1-13.

Jones, D. E. (1989). Library Support Staff and Technology. *Library Trends,* 37(4), 432-456.

Keefer, A., & Baiget, T. (2001). How it all Began: A Brief History of the Internet. *Vine,* 31(3), 90-91. DOI: 10.1108/03055720010804221

Khurshid, Z. (1998). ARABMARC: A Long Way to Go. *World Libraries,* 8(2), 60-68.

Kilgour, F. G. (1969). The Economic Goal of Library Automation. *College and Research Libraries,* 30(4), 307-311.

Kim, H., Hyunsoo, C., Gichai, H., Byungju, M., & Chee-Hang, P. (1999). Correlation between Users' Characteristics and Preferred Features of Web-Based OPAC Evaluation. *ETRI Journal,* 21(4), 83-93.

Kreslins, K., O'Brein, A., & Smith, I. A. (1994). Online Public Access Catalogues in Latvia: Strategies for Subject Access. *International Information and Library Review,* 26, 31-50.

Kupersmith, J. (1992). Techno Stress and the Reference. *Reference Services Review*, 20, 9.

Kurmey, W. J. (1982). The Impact of Technology. *Cataloguing and Classification Quarterly*, 2(1/2), 45-55.

Line, M. B. (1972). Automation and the British Library. *Library Association Record*, 47(11), 213-215.

Lundeen, G., & Tenopir, C. (1984). Microcomputer based Library Catalogue Software. *Microcomputers for Information Management*, 1(3), 21- 228.

Malik, K. M. (1996). The Status of Library Automation in Pakistan. *Library Review*, 45(6), 36-42.

Malik, K. M. (1998, January). The Development of the LAMP (Library Automation and Management Program) Software for use in Developing Countries and its Marketing in Pakistan. *Program: Automated Library and Information Systems*, 32(1), 37-48.

Marmion, D. (1998). Facing the Challenge: Technology Training in Libraries. *Information Technology & Libraries*, 17(4), 216-218.

Marchant, M. R. (1989). Changing Management Techniques as Libraries Automate. *Library Trends*, 37(2), 469-483.

Martin, A. B. (1949). Tulsa Finds New Aid in Photographic Charging. *Library Journal*, 74, 1476.

Martin, M. J. (1992). Academic Libraries and Computing Centers: Opportunities for Leadership. *Library Administration and Management*, 6(2), 77-81.

Martin, M. S. (1994). The Changing Library Environment. *Library Trends*, 42, 478-489.

Massey-Burzio, V. (1999). The Rush to Technology: A View from Humanists. *Library Trends*, 47(4), 620-639.

Mcbride, R. B. (1983). The Past, Present and Future of a Cataloguer. *Technical Services Quarterly*, 1, 137-141.

McCrank, L. J. (1986). The Impact of Automation: Integrating Archival and Bibliographic Systems. *Journal of Library Administration*, 7, 61-98.

Mehtab, A., & Amita, (2008). Awareness and Use of OPACs in Five Delhi libraries. *The Electronic Library*, 26(1), 111-129.

Mendez, A. (1983). To What Extent is Scientific Information Automated in Spain. *Program*, 17(4), 193-203.

Montague, E. (1978). Automation and the Library Administrator. *Journal of Library Administration*, 11(4), 313-323.

Morales, E. (2000). The Future of Library: A View from Mexico. *New Library World,* 101(1157), 212.

Moscoso, P., & Malo, D. M. T. (1999). And after Automation What? Spanish Libraries & Challenge of Modernization. *Journal of Librarianship & Information Science,* 31(2), 111-119.

Oketunji, S. F. (2003). X-LIB PLUS: A Library Application Software for Libraries and Information Centers. *Library HiTech News,* 20(9), 26-29.

Olsgaard, J. N. (1985). Automation as a Socio-Organizational Agent of Change: An Evaluative Literature Review. *Information Technology & Libraries.* 4(March), 19-28.

Oyemankinde, A. (1979). Automation at Ibadan University Library. *Program,* 3(3), 143-146.

Palmini, C. C. (1994). The Impact of Computerization on Library Support Staff: A Study of Support Staff in Academic Libraries in Wisconsin. *College and Research Libraries,* 119-127.

Peake, D. G. (1981) Library Automation in Australia: The State of Art. *Program Automated Library and Information Systems,* 15(1), 11-23.

Preston, G. A. (1983). How will Automation affect Cataloguing Staff? *Technical Services Quarterly,* 1, 129-136.

Prince, B., & Burton, P. F. (1988). Changing Dimensions in Academic Library Structures: The Impact of Information Technology. *British Journal of Academic Librarianship,* 3, 67-81.

Rajgopalan, G. (1981). Computerized Book Acquisition. *Journal of Library and Information Science,* 6(2), 84-91.

Rayman, R. (1980). Automated Interlibrary Lending: An Undiagnosed Problem. *Scholarly Publishing,* 12, 3-11.

Research Libraries Group. (1978). Research Libraries Group goes for BALLOTS. *Library Journal,* 103, 916.

Richmond, P. (1981). Library Automation in the United States of America. *Program Automated Library and Information Systems,* 15(1), 24-37.

Rooks, D. C., & Thompson, L. L. (1988). The Impact of Automation on Technical Services. *Journal of Library Administration,* 9(1), 121-136.

Saffady, W. (1989). Library Automation: An Overview. *Library Trends,* 37(3), 273.

Sajjad U. R., & Reham, A. (2010). Integrated Systems Applications in Kuwait Academic Libraries. *The Electronic Library,* 28(6), 858-872.

Sani, A., & Tiamiyu, M. (2005). Evaluation of Automated Services in Nigerian Universities. *The Electronic Library,* 23(3), 274-288.

Saunders, L. (1996). Changing Technology Transforms Library Roles. *Computers in Libraries,* 16, 49.

Saxena, S. C., & Srivastava, R. K. (1998). Evaluation of Library Software Packages Available in India. *DESIDOC Bulletin of Information Technology,* 18(5), 11-12.

Shabahat, H., & Mehtab, A. (2007). Library Automation Software Packages in India: A Study of Cataloguing Modules of Alice for Windows, LibSys and Virtua. *Annals of Library and Information Studies,* 54, 146-151.

Smalley, T. N. (1994). Computer Systems in Libraries: Have We Considered the Tradeoffs? *Journal of Academic Libraries,* 12, 356-361.

Taler, I. (1982). Automated and Manual ILL: The Effectiveness and Success Rate. *Information Technology & Libraries,* 1, 277-280.

Tran, L. A. (2005). Diffusion of Community Information Networks in New Zealand Public Libraries: A Case Study. *New Library World,* 106 (5&6), 269-283.

Tseng, S., & Pin-dar, K. (2009). A Study on the Patronage of Intelligent Library: The Ximen Intelligent Library of the Taipei Public Library System. *New Library World,* 110(9/10), 410-429.

Tyre, L. (1995). Library Automation; It is all about Connections. *Technological Horizons in Education,* 23(3), 60.

Tyskevie, N. I. (1972). Mechanization and Automation of Information and Library Operations in the USSR and their Development Prospects. *UNESCO Bulletin for Libraries,* 26(5), 247- 252.

Veaner, A. B. (1979). Major Decision Points in Library Automation. *College and Research Libraries,* 31(5), 299-312.

Vernon, E. (1996). Decision-Making for Automation: Hebrew and Arabic Script Materials in the Automated Library. *Occasional Papers,* University of Illinois, Urbana: Graduate School of Library & Information Science, 205, 96.

Voight, M. J. (1956). The Trend Towards Mechanization. *Library Trends,* 5(2), 193-205.

Wallace, D. P., & Joan, G. (1989) Microcomputers in Libraries. *Library Trends,* 37(4), 288-289.

Woods, R. G. (1986). Library Automation in British Universities. *Program Automated Library and Information Systems,* 20(4), 359-381.

Werking, R. H. (1991). Automation in College Libraries. *College & Research Libraries,* 52, 117-123.

WLN Reports (1979). WLN Reports Beachhead Down Under. *LJ/ LSJ Hotline,* 8(4), 2.

Wong, W. S. (1992). Automation and Library Administration with Special Reference to US East Asian Collection. *Journal of Educational Media & Library Science,* 29(2), 113-126.

Woodsworth, A. (1988). Computing Centers and Libraries as Cohorts: Exploiting Mutual Strengths. *Journal of Academic Librarianship,* 9(4), 21-34.

Yorkovich, J. D. (2001). Lied Library: At the Forefront of Technology with 3M Digital ID Collection Management. *New Library World,* 102(6), 216- 220.

Zeng, L. (1991). Automation of Bibliographic Control for Chinese Materials in the United States. *International Library Review,* 23, 299-319.

Zorn, P., Logan, E., Murphy, T., & Williams, L. (1995). Migration to the Horizon Integrated Library System at the Park-Devis Pharmaceutical Research Library: Project Implementation and System Overview. *Library Software Review,* 14(3), 137-145.

ENCYCLOPEDIAS

Feather, J., & Sturges, R. P. (2003). *International Encyclopedia of Information and Library Science.* London: Roultledge.

Halsey, W. D. (1987). *Collier's Encyclopedia.* New York: Macmillan.

Henderson, H. (2004). *The Encyclopaedia of Computer Science and Technology.* New Delhi: Viva Books.

Holland, S. W. (2005). Automation of American Criminal Justice. In Mehdi Khosrow-Pour (Ed.), *Encyclopaedia of Information Science and Technology.* USA: Idea Group Reference.

Pandey, S. K. (Ed.). (1999). *Encyclopaedia of Library Automation Systems and Networks.* New Delhi: Anmol.

Rawat, P. P., & Kumar, T. (1992). *International Encyclopaedia of Information Technology and Library Science.* New Delhi: Castle Books.

The New Encyclopedia Britannica. (1973). Macropedia. Chicago: Encyclopedia Britannica.

The New Oxford American Dictionary. (2001). Oxford: Oxford University Press.

Wedgeworth, R. (1993). *World Encyclopedia of Library and Information Services.* Michigan: American Library Association.

Young, H. (Ed.). (1983) *The ALA Glossary of Library & Information Science.* Chicago: ALA.

CONFERENCE PROCEEDINGS

Armstrong, C., & Stella, K. (Eds.). (1985). *Information Technology in the Library/Information School Curriculum: An International Conference.* England: Gower. Available from http://cat.inist.fr/?aModele=afficheN&cpsidt=2896981

Eyre, J. (Ed.). (1990). *Computers in Libraries International 90: Proceedings of the Fourth Annual Conference on Computers in Libraries.* London: Meckler.

Jeevan, V. K. J., & Kumar, R. V. (2002). *Design of Indigenous Library Automation Software: Experiences of Central Library, IIT Kharagpur, Information Management in e-Libraries: Proceedings of the National Conference on Information Management in e-Libraries (IMeL).* New Delhi: Allied.

Karen, W. (1988, September 8-11) Computer Applications in East Asian Libraries: Current Status and Future Trends: *International Symposium on New Techniques and Applications in Libraries*, Xi'an, Chinese People's Republic. Xi'an, China: Xi'an Jiao Tong University.

Kaul, H. K., & Malhan, I. V. (Eds.). (2006). *Knowledge Library and Information Networking NACLIN 2006: Proceedings of the National Conservation on Knowledge, Library & Information Networking held at University of Jammu.* New Delhi: DELNET.

Mclean, N. (1981). Computerization and Library Organization. *The Management of Technical Innovations in Libraries: Proceedings of a Conference.* Loughborough: Center for Library and Information Management.

Schnelling, H. (1992, November 23-26). Management Issues in

Library Automation: Experiences from German University Libraries. *Paper Presented at the EEC Comet Course, University Libraries and Information Transfer: Automation as New Organizational Language*. Venice.

Thompson, R. K. H. (1992, September 13-17). *Funding for Library Automation: Paper Presented at the National Conference of the Library and Information Technology Association (3rd)*. Denver.

Vashishth, C. P. (Ed.) (1988, December 28-31). *Modernization in Libraries: Proceedings of Seminar Papers Thirty-third All India Library Conference Bharathidaran University,* Tiruchirapalli. Delhi: Indian Library Association.

Wayne, D. (1972). *Mini Computers and Library Automation: The Standard Experience: Proceedings of the 1974 Clinic on Library Applications and Data Processing.* Urbana, III: University of Illinois Graduate School of Library science.

WEBSITES

Amaraweera, J.A. (2002). Automation of Library Operations in Sri Lanka: Cost Effective Web based Solution. *Information Development,* 18(2), 111- 116. Available from http://idv.sagepub.com/content/18/2/111.full.pdf+html

Bharduwaj, R., & Shukla, R. K. (2000). *Library Automation; A Practical Approach to Library Automation.* Chicago: Library of Congress, 20(1), 1-9. Available from http://drtc.isibang.ac.in/bitstream/handle/1849

Breeding, M. (2002). *Association of Research Libraries: Current Automation Systems.* Available from http://www.library technology.org/arl.pl

Clinkenbeard, A. (2007) *Library Automation Considerations.* Available from http://www.widernet.org/sites/default/files/LibraryAutomation.pdf

Francis, A. T. (1998). Software Problems in Library Automation in India. *Information Management in Academic and Research Libraries,* 60-64. Available from http://eprints.rclis.org/bitstream/10760/7425/1/CALIBER.98_Software.

Freedman, M. J. (1976). The Automation of Cataloguing. *Library Trends,* 703-721. Available from http://www.ideals.illinois.edu/bitstream/handle/2142/8767/librarytrendsv25i3j_opt.pdf?sequence=2

Freedman, M. J. (1984). Automation and Future of Technical

Services. *Library Journal,* 1197-1203. Available from http://www.mjfreedman.org/articles/alts.html.

Intuitive Products International. (2011). *A Brief History of Library Automation, Research Papers.* Available from http://www.Justfreepapers.com/papers/15926/abriefhistoryoflibraryaut

McCallum, S. H. (2002). MARC: Keystone for Library Automation. *IEEE Annals of the History of Computing,* Library of Congress, 45-47. Available from http://www.ieeeexplore.ieee.org/iels

Qiang, Z. (2007). *The Development of Library Automation in Peking University.* Beijing: Peeking University. Available from http://web.simmons.edu/~chen/nit/NIT'92/411-zhu.htm

Savage, C. M. (1996). *Fifth Generation Management: Co-creating through Virtual Enterprising, Dynamic Teaming, and Knowledge Networking.* (Rev. 2nd ed.). Woburn: Butterworth-Heinemann. Available from http://Books.google.co.in/books?id

Singley, Y. (1998). *Status Report on Library Automation and Networking in Community Colleges.* Available from http://www.lib.niu.edu/1998/il980129.html www.kashmiruniversity.net/.html

www.library.iitd.ac.in/index.html

www.library.iitk.ac.in/index.html

www.inflibnet.ac.in

www.libsys.co.in/home.html.

www.softlinkasia.com.au

www.ugc.ac.in

www.vtls.com/products/virtua.

Index

E

F

G

H